T0365905

MY STORY

AMY RICHARDSON

authorHOUSE®

AuthorHouse™
1663 Liberty Drive
Bloomington, IN 47403
www.authorhouse.com
Phone: 833-262-8899

Published by AuthorHouse 06/16/2021

ISBN: 978-1-6655-2921-1 (sc)
ISBN: 978-1-6655-2922-8 (e)

THE AMAZING
FIRST DATE

have the excitement and anticipation of not knowing what to wear. I have not been on a real date in like forever. My heart is beating so fast and the dizziness I feel in my head makes me feel like a teenager all over again. I don't even know where he is taking me, but he does know that I love Country music. After spending five years living in Kentucky it has grown on me.

Okay,....I'm going country tonight. I go into my closet and search for the perfect outfit. I pull out my adorable matching purple and white flowered top and flaring skirt. The skirt twirls out when I spin around. I find the white cowgirl boots to accent it. I have some gold hoop earrings to show a little flash. I am going to look hot tonight. I doll up my makeup and make sure my eyelashes are long and curled. I have been told many times that I have sexy bedroom eyes. It's time to bring these babies out. My long hair needs to be fluffed and full. I highlighted it recently so the sandy blonde tints should shine through beautifully. I bend over and flip my head back up to get the perfect fluff and spray the hairspray evenly. Now I gently place the white matching cowgirl hat on my head. A few shots of Estee Lauder's beautiful and I'm an ready for action.

It's almost 6:00, the babysitter is here, and the girls are nestled on the couch under their favorite blanket watching Rugrats. My heart is beating a million miles a minute waiting for him to get here. I don't know what it is about him, but when he looks into my eyes I just melt. I have received one card with flowers each day this week. I can't remember the last time I felt so special and admired. I feel so young and full of life. I feel happy again for once.

I hear the engine of his corvette coming around the corner. This is it. "Girls, mommy will be back in a while. Listen to Alexa and don't give her a hard time tonight." "Mommy, you look so pretty", replied my zesty little blonde 3 year old daughter. If she didn't have her older sister and a friend to play with right now, she would never let me out the door. She is my clingy daughter. From the day she was born we have been joined at the hip. My older daughter Julienne is much more independent, stubborn, and can be quite defiant when she doesn't get her way. She is a dare devil like her father. He wasn't much of a dad when he needed to be. He loved the bottle and parties more than his family most of the time. His irresponsible behavior of seven years finally took its toll and encouraged me to move on. I want more and I want to be happy. I deserve better and so do my girls.

I look out the window and there he is. He walks up the steps to meet me. I open the door to see his charming smile. This man is not shy. He gives me a wink and asks, "Are you ready gorgeous?" I smile back, give him my are arm, and off we go.

His car is magnificently clean. It has white leather seats that smell brand new. He opens the door for me and I sit down while he runs to the other side. He is dressed in sexy jeans with boots and a blue button down shirt. His cologne is tranquilizing. Smells like Eternity I believe. God I'm am in heaven. He looks over at me and shakes his head. "What?" I ask with a cute smile. "You are so beautiful. I am the luckiest man alive right now" He cranks the stereo. It's the 1990's and Matchbox Twenty is playing. I feel free.

"Where are we going?" I ask him with anticipation. "I can't tell you that. It's a surprise. But, only the best for you." he says as he shifts gears and then gently grabs my hand. He brings my hand to his lips and so gently kisses it and then turns to wink at me. How romantic is this? I swear I am creaming my panties at this moment. When have I last felt like this? He is so charming and so sexy.

We pull into a parking lot that runs along the river. It's beautiful. There are winding trails and boat docks everywhere. We park and then he leans over and kisses me so softly. "Are you ready?" he asks as I stare at him in a trance wanting more I finally reply back, "Yes." He walks around the car and opens the door for me. We walk up the long set of steps to the restaurant doors. The restaurant is classy. There are white table cloths, dinner music playing in the background, and wait staff walking around in proper uniform attire. "Mr. Richardson, I see you have made it, right this way." says the hostess. She walks us over to our table. The view is incredible. We are looking out at the water and all of the boaters going by. Candles are lit at our table. A waiter comes to the table and says, "Here is the wine that you requested sir ready for you to enjoy." Wow, I'm amazed. I know he has money and all, but I guess he has a lot of pull too. Well he is a business man.

I order my steak and lobster just like him. He poured our glasses of wine and made sure that he had also ordered me a vodka and cranberry to go with my dinner. He knew from previous conversations that it was my favorite cocktail. "You are so beautiful" he says to me. "God, I can't believe that I have you here with me right now. We are going to have an amazing night."

Dinner is over. He leaves a hefty tip and says to me, "Come on, let's go have some fun." Back in the car he spins his tires to be cool and silly and then cranks the stereo and sings to me. I can't help but laugh and grin from ear to ear. I want to spend the rest of my life with this man. It doesn't get any better than this. We arrive at the country western bar outside of town. I can hear the band outside. Oh this is going to be so much fun. I love to dance. I hope he does too.

We get inside and get settled at the bar. This place is rocking. I have one sip and before I know it, he whips me away onto the dance floor. I love this kind of spontaneity. It makes my heart throb. Garth Brook's "Low Places" is playing. We sing to each other dramatizing the words and dancing away with huge smiles on our faces. Now it's time for a slow dance. John Berry's "Your love amazes me" is being played. He grabs me close and we dance heart to heart. He pulls away to look at my face. His beautiful blue eyes look into mine. I'm in love just like that. He gently cups my face in his hands and kisses me. I want to be lost in this moment forever.

It's time to leave. We walk back to the car. It's two o'clock in the morning. He asks me, "Did you have a good time?" I smiled and shook my head with a definite yes. "I love you Amy"

MEETING OF
THE GIRLS

"I have my daughter this weekend. We should spend a weekend together like a family and let the girls get to know each other" Nick tells me. "I have to work some, but I have plenty of room here at the house so they can play and get comfortable being around each other." I do love the idea. Things having been going so great between us and my daughters really do seem to like him. Of course he does spoil them just a little. He did buy them new bikes and new outfits. He took them to Chucky Cheese while I was working. They road along with him to work so he could show them off and would take them out for ice cream afterwards. I mean, what kid wouldn't like him? He loves spending time with my girls and that warms my heart. Their own father has never been one to spend time with them. He also moved away to Arizona with his parents since our divorce. My girls need a good dad in their lives to love them and spend time with them. Nick could very well be that man. "Yes that sounds awesome." I say "I'll take all of the girls to Michael's craft store to pick out some projects that we can all do together." "Enough said" as he smiles and pulls out a couple hundred dollar bills out of his pocket to give to me. "Will that be enough? Do you need money for gas and food?" he asked. And before I could say another word he pulled out another hundred. It takes me a week to make that sometimes. "I don't want you to worry about money anymore." he says "Later tonight we are going to talk about you no longer cleaning other people's houses. I don't want my baby killing herself like this anymore. You deserve to be able to be a mom and have a man take care of you for a change." Hearing these words from him is so inviting. Is this for real? Can I really live the dream of being an at home mom with a husband who takes care of us financially and actually plays the role of a father in the home. I look into his eyes and tears of gratitude fall from mine. He hugs me close, smiles with a chuckle, and off he goes. "See ya later tonight honey!" he yells as he runs down to his work van.

While the girls are out back on the swing set, I walk through this huge house in wonder. I'm not a greedy person by any means, but knowing this could be mine and giving my children a better life is overwhelming. We can all live here. A big beautiful house, a large yard here out in the country to play in, and most importantly stability with all of their financial needs met. I picture them being able to run, play, and giggle. And, I will get to be here all of the time to witness it. I don't want to be so tired anymore. I want to be a better mom.

The girls and I decide to get a snack and unwind to a movie on the big screen in the living room while we wait for Nick's return. "Mommy it's really fun here." says Jessica "What do you think of this place Julienne?" I ask. She's a little more hesitant to answer, but then says "It's pretty cool."" Nick and I have a big surprise for you guys tonight." Their eyes light up. "Really, like what?" Jessica asks. "You will see very soon." Five minutes later we hear the front door open.

"Hi honey. We are home!" I noticed he said WE. It's Nick and his daughter Marley. She is an adorable blonde hair, blue eyed little four year old girl. She is literally in between the ages of my girls. How perfect is that? They come into the living room to greet us. "Surprise!" I say to my girls. "This is Marley." "Marley why don't you show Julienne and Jessica your room." Nick says with a wink to me. And before we know it we hear the footsteps of three little girls running back and forth laughing and screaming with joy upstairs. They all hit it off immediately.

"We are going to one of Marley's favorite places tonight. Get ready for a great dinner." He tells me as he looks at me and holds me in front of him. "You just wait. This is only the beginning" he says. "But what about me taking the girls to the craft store?" "Worry about it tomorrow" he answers. "Do I need to change my clothes? I'm in a T-shirt and shorts. I feel I need to go home and freshen up." "It's up to you" he says. "I'll look after the girls. Go grab some overnight bags and take whatever time that you need for yourself. I'll make reservations for 7:00." He just smiles and winks at me. "I got this. They will be fine. Go." I'm in awe. *How* can I say no. I feel so special and spoiled.

MOVED IN AND
I'M PREGNANT

essica and Marley decided that they want to share their bedroom while Julienne decided that she wants her own bedroom for privacy and space. They are opening all of their boxes of belongings and decorating their new rooms with pride. I feel good about our decision to move in. It's been a couple months of pretty much staying here all of the time anyway. We love being here. I am so in love with Nick. Yes this is our new home and our new future.

I did not have much to move. I sold as much as I could furniture wise. The girl's dad left me in such a financial mess. I used the money I made off the furniture for other necessities. So actually moving here was quite easy. Nick's home and Nick things, is now our home and our things. I no longer work or have to worry about anything.

Marley is staying with us more and more now since I am home to take care of her. It gives her mom a break and she loves being with the girls. Nick makes sure that I always have plenty of cash to keep them busy during the day. He gets babysitters often to give me a break and take me out of the house. I go to work with him a lot, and then it's out for a romantic dinner, cocktails, and making love in the car. When he has a good day in sales he wants to celebrate. It's his high in life. He works very hard. He takes me shopping and we even made love in the changing room. It's never boring.

Cars are going by and it's dusk. We are parked on a country road. We are making out in the Jeep Cherokee. His hands are now going down my pants. God, I'm paralyzed every times he gets to this point. "What do you want honey? Should I stop?" He says as he is now fingering me. I want him so bad right here and right now. I'm breathless and my body is arching. I'm moaning. "Ah ah, my naughty girl wants more." He opens his door and runs over to mine. He opens my door, pulls me out of the car, turns me around, pulls down my pants, and bends me over. He takes a quick look around for cars, opens his pants, and enters me with his swollen penis. It feels incredible. I come instantly. This is a high that I have never experienced. It's so spontaneous, intoxicating, naughty, and invigorating. "Oh my God!" I yell as we both come together. I can't believe I climaxed again so quickly. We both get back in the car quickly laughing and breathing hard. "Where should we do it next time?' he asks giggling.

We make love as often as we can and everywhere that we can. I can't get in the shower without him following me in there. I am on the pill. Having a baby with him would probably be a beautiful thing, but a little soon. Hell we are not even married and we are having a lot of fun right now. I keep my birth control pills on the downstairs bathroom sink so that I don't forget to take them each night. There has been a couple times when I have questioned my taking them. My pill would be gone for that day, but I couldn't pinpoint when I took it. Today is another one of those days. I feel like I'm losing my mind. I shrug it off. We are on the go often and I am probably just spacing it out.

It's a chilly morning and I just dread crawling out of this warm bed. The alarm clock is beeping and it's 6:30 am. Our house is a little drafty in the cooler months seeing that half the house is over a hundred years old and not well insulated. Nick has already left for work. He is an early bird. He only sleeps about five hours a night. I work my way out of bed to head down to Julienne's room and then the whirl of dizziness and nausea hits me. I dash to the bathroom with dry heaves. Well this is great. I must have a tummy bug. Now I have to worry about all of the kids getting it next. But, I am not achy. I have been very tired this last week. My period is two weeks late. It does happen to me sometimes. Oh no, this can't be. I'm on the pill. I'm sick that's all.

I get Julienne off to school. She had cereal while the girls slept. The smells in the kitchen are making me want to hurl as I'm trying to put last night's dishes in the dishwasher. The phone rings. "Hey honey, how we doing today?" Nick asks all chipper. "Horrible" I manage to say. "What's wrong?" "I'm so nauseated." I reply. "Did you get your period yet?" he asks. It's funny that is the first thing that he asks. "No, but I'm on the pill. It can't be that. It must be a bug." "Honey you know the pill is not one hundred percent. Maybe I should pick you up a pregnancy test." "Do whatever you want. I'm crawling back in bed." I replied.

One half hour later I hear him running up the stairs to the bedroom. "Look what I got ya honey!" He says with excitement in his voice. He hands me the pregnancy test. He must obviously want me to be pregnant. I sit up, look into those beautiful eyes of his and say, "Okay, here goes." I'm off to the bathroom to pee on the famous stick that can change someone's life forever. I sit on the toilet and wait. Maybe this could be a good thing. He and I could be bringing a new life into this world out of true love. It's been three minutes. I'm afraid to look. I stand up and walk my way over to the sink. I look down. I can't believe my eyes. I'm pregnant. Nick walks in and stands behind me. He looks down and sees the result. I watch his expression as he looks back at me in the mirror. His smile couldn't be any bigger. He turns me around, kisses me, and says two words, "Marry me." "Yes Yes!" I say "I will marry you!" as the tears of happiness fell from both of our eyes.

THE FIRST SIGN

he girls take the news really well. They are actually showing a lot of excitement and want to know who is going to be responsible for what at the wedding. We plan to make them a big part of everything. Nick and I can't wait to share all of our good news with our family and friends. We have only been together three months, but this all feels so right.

We finish up dinner and while I am cleaning up the phone rings. I answer "Hello". "Amy it's Jennifer. I need to talk to Nick." Jennifer is Marley's mom. She sounds very angry and impatient. "Sure hold on." I reply. Nick takes the phone into the other room and before I know it we all hear him yelling at the top of his lungs. "Ya I pay you plenty for Marley. I don't like you sending her here in dirty clothes and not bathed. She tells me that she is up late with you all of the time and lives on McDonalds. Jesus Jennifer you don't even know how to take care of her. Yes I'm getting married and having another child. Marley likes it here and she wants to call Amy Mom so be it. She is one hell of a better mother than you will ever be. I want custody!" He slams the phone down so hard the receiver cracked in half. I can't believe what I just heard. This is not him. He is being so cruel. She is Marley's mother and Marley loves her. "I'm going for a ride. I need to go sell a deal and cool down." He says. I get no kiss, no hug and out the door with a huge slam behind him he goes. I hear his tires peel out of the drive way. I have never seen him this angry or act in this manner. It's really scary. The girls are stunned and are frozen stiff in the kitchen.

I am still dealing with nausea and vomiting and his little blow up with Jennifer sure has not helped the situation. The girls run over to me, hug me and Jessica asks, "Why was Nick yelling like that? Is he mad at you?" She is always so sweet and innocent not to mention concerned about others. "No honey. He just had an argument with Marley's mom." "But, why?" Julienne asks "He sounded so mad." "I'm not really sure right now." I say "I will talk to him later when calms down. Don't worry. Everything will be fine. Mommy has an upset tummy so I'm going to lay down for a bit. Can you guys get ready for bed and watch a movie please?"

An hour passes and he is back. He is in a very happy mood. Talk about Jeckle and Hyde. He comes upstairs to our bedroom were I'm somewhat asleep and says "I'm sorry you heard me yelling like that. She just knows how to push my buttons and all she wants from me is money." Now he is all over me with no romance involved. I don't feel well and this is the last thing that I feel like doing. I open my mouth to tell him not now and he is already inside me pumping hard. "God I love you." he says and then he screams as he orgasms. Then he lays next to me. "Do you need anything honey?" he asks. I sit up, cover my mouth, and run to the bathroom. I made it just in time. I brush my teeth, drink some water, and beg God to make this morning sickness go away. I just sit there on the bathtub and think. How does he change like a light switch so quickly? And what was that all about? I feel so used right now.

The vomiting continues and I have not been able to keep anything down for two days. I think stress is making things worse. We get Nick's mother to come stay with the kids and we head to the hospital. I am very dehydrated. I'm told that I have hyperemesis and I need to spend a night in the hospital on intravenous fluids. Well it's not the first time that I have had to do this. I went through the same thing with my other pregnancies. Nick stays with me until after dinner time talking on his phone most of the time of course. He is telling everyone about my condition. I swear he likes to get attention whenever he can. He has to be the center of attention. "Say some prayers for us that we don't lose the baby." I hear him say to someone. Seriously, I'll be home tomorrow. We were already told that the baby is fine. He gets off the phone, pulls the privacy curtain so nobody can see from outside our room. He lays in bed with me and giggles. "Let's do it here in the hospital. This would be such a cool memory to have." He slides his hands down my panties and starts fingering me. I move his hand away and turn my back to him. The next thing I know he is penetrating me with his penis from behind. "Nick, please stop this. Someone may come in here. I don't feel good for God's sake.

What is wrong with you?" "Hold still just a second more." He comes inside me. Not five minutes later the nurse walks in sees him lying in bed with me. "How sweet that your man cuddles with you in the hospital." She says. God if she only knew.

Finally after another two weeks of hell I am feeling like myself again. I start getting everything planned for our simple wedding that's only six weeks away. I don't want to be a fat pregnant woman on my wedding day so we have moved things along at a quick pace. Our reception is going to be here at home so it will be easy on the kids as well. I am going today to pick out my wedding dress. I will be taking all of the girls with me and then we are going to find their dresses as well. It's going to be a girl's day. We are going to have a lot of fun. It will really make them feel a part of everything.

Nick has been back to his normal self as well. I think me being so sick was a little rough on everyone. We are all happy to be back in the groove, excited for our new life together as a family. The little shout out he had with Jennifer is long done and over with. Maybe she really does have some issues and needed to be put in her place. It's none of my business anyway.

OFFICIALLY
HUSBAND AND WIFE

e are husband and wife. My belly is growing. We can feel the baby kicking now. The little thuds tickle like butterflies fluttering in my stomach. I do miss these days of carrying a baby. I know these tickles are going to change into real feet protruding across my tummy knocking my bowls of snacks over. Nick talks to my tummy every day. He rubs it softly. "You have a beautiful Mommy." He tells his unborn child as he lays his head gently on my abdomen. He loves my body. He loves me. He makes me feel so special and beautiful. He takes my picture all of the time. He shows me off in public with pride.

It's the day of the ultrasound. Are we having a boy or a girl? We hold each other's hand in the doctor's office while the wand is circling my tummy. "There he is on the screen." says the doctor. Nick is over joyed. We are having a boy. "I'm going to have a son." He cries out. He kisses me, "I love you so much Amy. Thank you." I am giving him a son.

What I am now learning is that all of the bliss of this relationship is wearing off quickly. I'm at home with three girls all of the time running a house while my Nick is nowhere ever to be found. For the third time this afternoon I try his cell phone only to get his voicemail. I have not heard from him since he left early this morning. I leave a message. "Hi, hey remember me? Will you be here for dinner to even help tuck the girls in? It would be nice to hear from you." This is becoming quite a routine lately. I'm feeling some loneliness these days. He tells me he has so much work to get done and he is sorry.

The girls and I eat our mac and cheese, watch Cone Heads together, and then I send them up to their rooms for bed. "When is my dad coming home? He is never here." Marley asks as she crawls into her bed. "I miss my mom." I can't blame her. She has not seen her mom in a month. Nick tells her she is busy working and tells me she is busy partying. "Marley is better off here with us." He tells me. I am her full time mom now. "It's late, but how about we call her in the morning." I say to her to try to ease her frustration. "She's up. We stay up late all of the time and cuddle. Can I call her now?" She asks as she starts to cry. I figure we can try. I'll call to see if she answers first.

I dial the number and wait. "Hello." I hear on the other end. "Hi Jennifer." "Yes?" she asks in anticipation. "It's Amy, Marley is here asking to talk to you before she goes to sleep tonight. Is that okay?" "Oh my God yes of course! Please put her on now!" Wow I think as I hand the phone over to Marley. What in the world is going on here? Nick has made it sound like she doesn't give a damn about the kid. "Mommy, when can I come home? I miss you so much." Marley cries her heart out to her mother. "But Daddy said you had to work a lot right now so I have to stay here." She is quiet while her mother is talking on the other line. "He's not home; only Amy."

And now it begins. Marley gives me the phone. "My mom wants to talk to you." I can hear Jennifer crying on the other end before she speaks. "Amy, you have no idea what you are in for or what Nick is really all about. This is not my choice to be away from my daughter. He is in total control of this situation. You are the only reason that I know she is safe right now. He comes over here every night trying to fuck me and then threatens to kill me if I come near our daughter right now. He is so sick. He has tried to kill me before. He has choked me until I turned blue while sitting on top of me. He stalks me, threatens me, and holds money from me. I'm terrified to be telling you this. Please don't tell him that I told you any of this. I want my daughter back home. I just don't know how to go about getting her back here. We have no legal arrangement and I can't afford a lawyer."

I just sit there not knowing what to say. Could any of this be true? This all sounds so extreme and crazy. I can't picture him being this way. And why in the world would he want to sleep with her? He can't stand her. After the way they argued on the phone that one night I just can't see it. I need to talk to him. He is my husband. "Jennifer I will talk to Nick about letting Marley go back home. She obviously misses you very much. I don't understand why he can't take a step back and be reasonable. He will listen to me. Don't worry." I tell her before we say our goodbyes. And, I could really use the break myself.

The kids are sound asleep and I'm still restless. I can't stop thinking about everything Jennifer said. I turn to look at the clock and it reads 11:06 p.m. I can't fall asleep not knowing where he is. He has not answered my calls. I get out of bed and walk over to the window. Our master bedroom sits on top of our three car garage. It's snowing outside. The outside driveway is lit up and glistening from the snow flakes. I look for fresh tire treads. There are none. Where can he be? My thoughts are starting to make me crazy especially after that phone conversation with Jennifer. Something is not right. I can feel it in my gut.

I have to rest for the baby's sake. I lye back down and try to relax. My heart is racing, my stomach is upset, I'm shaky, and I feel like I'm losing my mind. At some point I must have finally dozed off. I turned over to see my husband lying down next to me as the sun is rising. He is out cold and snoring quite loudly which he doesn't usually do. I smell the booze coming from his breath. I feel so angry and hurt right now. What is going on? This man couldn't stand to spend a minute away from me before. I push him hard and yell at him with tears coming out of my eyes. "Where the hell have you been?" He sits up disoriented and a second later he's off running to the bathroom to vomit. Lovely, I think to myself. As I turn my head I notice blood on his pillow. Maybe he hurt himself on top of everything else. I went to the bathroom to check on him and that's when I notice the blood running out of his nose. "Jesus, are you okay?" I ask. "Ya, I'm fine." He says as he kneels over the toilet bowl. "You're bleeding." I say. "I must have a dry nose from my allergies. We should get a humidifier put through the house." He says. "When did you get home last night?" I was worried and now smelling the booze oozing out of him quite pissed off too. "What's going on with you?" I press on in frustration. "I had an aggravating day and didn't want to bring it home." "You couldn't call me? I've been worried sick!" I yell. "How the hell would you feel if I did this to you?"

I just pushed one of his buttons. I could see the rage in his eyes glaring back at me. "Everything I fucking do for you and your kids. I can come and go when I want!" I just stood there in shock. The tears are building. Why is he talking to me like this? I turn away and go back to the bed and cry my heart out. Who is this man? He is not the man that I fell in love with. Maybe Jennifer was telling the truth. He then cleans himself up, no apologies, and goes downstairs to sleep with his daughter.

With swollen eyes I walk my way downstairs a few hours later to the sound of family laughter. Nick has cooked a big breakfast for the girls and has them all excited about getting out on the snowmobiles today. We had a large snowfall last night and the trails around here are fresh and ready to go. I just look at him and wonder if he has any remorse about last night. He is acting like nothing ever happened. He is all happy and full of energy.

"Hi Honey." He say. "I made ya some breakfast." He says with his wink and charming smile. Is he trying to say that he is sorry? "You need to rest, eat, and take care of our baby." What the fuck, I am so confused. Talk about dealing with Mr. Jeckle and Mr. Hyde.

"Mommy, Nick is taking us in the sleigh!" Jessica says out loud joyfully with giggles. "It's going to be so much fun!" Marley joins in. Julienne seems excited too, but doesn't jump in with them. I can tell she senses something is not right with me. I'm sure she notices my swollen eyes and knows that I have been crying. She also knows that Nick was sleeping with Marley. She is very observant being the oldest.

"Okay girls, scrape your dishes and go get all of your gear together." Nick says as he smiles at me. The girls do as they are told and take off running with excitement. "Take some time for yourself honey. Get some rest. You look tired." He says to me. Ya no shit I think to myself. I wonder why. "Nick we need to talk about Jennifer later. It's really important." I can see in his eyes that this is not a good time to bring this up. But when is it for God's sake? I wanted to talk to him last night. "Marley wants to go home" I tell him with compassion in my voice hoping he will listen. "Does it look like she wants to go home right now? She looks pretty damn happy to me." He replied in agitation. "We gotta go. Come on kids! The trails are waiting!"

What the hell is wrong with him? He is so damn edgy. I can't just have a conversation with him anymore. I need to talk to somebody. I feel so alone, sad, angry, and I really want a damn cigarette right now. I don't see many of my friends living out here in the country anymore. Nick always wants me close by. I do have one high school friend close by. I walk into the kitchen, pick up our landline phone, and dial Carol's number. Maybe she will be home today and I can come by. I need to get out of here before I lose my mind. "Hello." She answers. "Hi girlfriend." I say. "What are you doing on this blistery day?" "Hi Amy. I'm not going anywhere if I don't have to." She said with her usual laugh. "I'm trying to get some housework done if anything." "Do you mind if I come over?" I ask. "Sure, is everything okay? Do you have the girls with you?" I hesitate for a moment, but then just tell her that I need some company and somebody to talk to. "Nick took the girls snowmobiling." "I'll make us some coffee and muffins, come on over bitch." She says with her goofy laugh. I really miss the company of a good friend.

After spending a couple hours at Carol's pouring my heart out to her, I felt a little weight off my shoulders. Just to tell her how powerless I feel and how worried I am that I made a mistake marrying Nick. She agreed that the way he is treating me mentally is very wrong, unhealthy, and that I am not crazy. "Don't put up with it Amy. You don't deserve this. You are carrying his child for God's sake." She gave me some inner strength back. I felt support, loved, and ready to put Nick in his place if his behavior continues.

I walk into the house. It's a ghostly quiet. They are not back yet. This is a good time to take a nice hot shower. I need some tranquil time just for me. The heat is beating on my skin, soothing my neck and shoulders, and I'm finally feeling some relaxation. I'm washing my hair and then I hear Nick's voice loud and clear telling the girls to change and to get settled upstairs in their rooms for a while. The bathroom door opens and I hear, "Hey honey, I'm home. Oh yes she is ready for me." Oh God I think to myself. I just want to be left alone. He rips his clothes off quickly and hops in the shower with me. I don't even get a kiss or caress. He turns me around and starts fucking me from behind. It's over in less than a minute. "Thanks baby. God I love that ass of yours." He says to me, hops back out, and on his way he goes just like that. The girls are now knocking on the bathroom door calling for me. I feel used. I travel outside of my body while I stare back at myself in the mirror. I'm numb. "I'll be out soon guys. Please give mommy a few minutes. "Mom, we have money. Nick said we can all go shopping and to Chucky Cheese." I can hear them jumping up and down and giggling. Then I hear their footsteps run down the hallway. My tears pour down my face. Well this is how I get paid for a good fuck. I dry my eyes and get myself together.

I walk into the living room to see that they are watching cartoons. "Hey guys. Where did Nick go?" "He had to go back to work." Marley says. Then I look over at Julienne sitting by herself at the opposing couch. She does not appear excited or happy. She is very quiet just looking down at her lap twiddling with her fingers. Hmm, I wonder if she just feels left out because Jessica and Marley take to each other so well. She must be feeling left out.

I head up stairs and get myself dressed. It's time for me to look human and hide these swollen eyes once again. I am very tired no doubt, but maybe a fun day out with the girls will do me some good. I dress in some cute comfortable clothes and head back downstairs to the living room. "Okay guys lets go have some fun!" I say in a chipper voice. Instantly the girls get up and run to get their coats and shoes and out the door we went.

WELCOME TO YOUR NEW HOME TYLER

y belly is rapidly growing. The seasons have changed. It's getting so hot outside. Being pregnant and heat do not mix very well. The girls and I do more and more things alone. I never know where Nick is. When I call his office I'm always told he is out working. He never answers when I call his cell phone. You would think he would be waiting for my calls being this pregnant. He comes home at all hours of the night. I have Marley a lot of the time. I am basically raising her. Her mother is now partying a lot with her friends. I guess things change. Maybe she gave up on being that great mom or she is taking advantage of knowing I'm doing a great job taking care of her. Jennifer was pregnant right out of high school so she never lived the fun single life without a kid. Well, she sure is now. I am starting to feel so lonely and depressed. I'm tired all of the time and uncomfortable from being pregnant. The only time that Nick has time for me is when I tell him that I'm going to see my family. You see he doesn't want me to reach out to receive any kind of love or support from my friends or loved ones. This is when he drops everything to take me out to eat or something. He does not mind if I go to see his mother of course. Hell, he even pays me to go clean her house. She is a hoarder. It's impossible to clean her house. I don't want to clean her house. She babies Nick and thinks he's the greatest thing in the world. Little does she know the truth of what her son is like behind closed doors.

When Nick occasionally gets me out of the house he likes to bring me to the office to show me off to his coworkers by rubbing my belly being the proud daddy to be. I actually do feel some attention and special during these moments. I'm in my ninth month. Nick is very proud that I have only gained twenty pounds total from the pregnancy. From my back side you don't even know that I'm pregnant. I just have this little basketball coming out of the front of me.

In the last week or so Nick suddenly has an obsession with my body. This sexual attraction towards me took over. I feel good again. Wow, he does love me. I did not experience this with my ex-husband. He was turned off by my pregnancies and wouldn't even look at or touch me. "You are so beautiful." He tells me. He takes my picture all of the time and makes love to me regularly. And I do mean making love, not just having sex. He is taking me out to nice restaurants again and even makes sure we are moved up in line telling hostesses "My wife is pregnant with low blood sugar." He takes me to work on sales calls again and stops regularly to get me snacks and juice. He takes the girls out to dinner or hires babysitters to give me breaks so I can rest. He sends me on shopping sprees for the baby. I feel like a princess once again. He's getting himself back together. Our son will be here soon. Things are going to be good.

Before I head up to bed at night I usually check on the girls to make sure that they are settled down or sleeping. This week four nights in a row out of the blue Julienne is wetting herself in her sleep. I can smell the urine when I walk in the bedroom and as soon as I lean over her I know that it is her. I feel the bed and it's soaked. All four nights I wake her and we change her bedding, wipe her down, and put on clean clothing. What in the world is going on? It's the next morning and I decide that she needs to see the doctor. She might have a urinary tract infection. The doctor checks her urine and tells me it's negative for any bacteria. "This happens to some kids from time to time. Is there any stress in the home or with her friends?" he asks me. I think to myself that it's not great, but lately it's been pretty good. "We have a baby about to be born. Maybe that has something to do with it." I say.

I stop her liquid consumption at night to see if that helps. I have not told Nick about this. I do not want to bother him with it. Now I'm finding dirty underwear hidden in her room. I finally talk to a specialist about a device that we can attach to her at night to wake her when she has to go. She sleeps so soundly that it doesn't even work. One night in very late pregnancy when I'm completely exhausted after checking on her, Nick hears us upstairs. He decides to take over. "Why is she peeing the bed? She is too old for this. This mattress is going to get ruined." He woke her and dragged her to the bathtub while yelling at her. Julienne is half asleep. I follow behind them in distress. The water is still running, but there is enough water in the tub. He takes her clothes off and lifts her into the tub. Julienne is crying. She is cold and scared. I stand there frozen for a minute. "Nick please just chill out. She is scared." I said. "I'll change the sheets so we can get her back to bed.

Julienne who is now 32 years old swears to this day that Nick fondled her at this time. Julienne is my child that acted out against him over the years and did take the most abuse from him. I don't want to believe this to this day, but now that I go back and look at the situation these were my first signs to realize what was happening between Julienne and Nick.

It's my last doctor's appointment. The birth is going to be scheduled during the Boone County Fair. This time of the year is the busiest time for Nick to be working of course. On August fifteenth our pride and joy will be here. I'm hoping Nick can be prepared to be there too. He better be. I'll be damned if I am going to go through this alone.

We check into the hospital at seven a.m. I am due to be induced at nine a.m. We both sit in the hallway waiting for the hospital staff to take me back to my room. We are both excited and nervous. I'm scared of labor pains once again. I know that I did this twice already, but I also know that this is still going to hurt like hell. I hope that I dilate quickly and get that epidural as soon as possible.

It's been only six hours and it's time for this bundle of joy to arrive. Nick has been taking pictures of me this whole time. He even has the staff take pictures of him cutting the cord. A six pound thirteen ounce baby boy named Tyler Richardson is now a part of this world. Nick is one very proud daddy. He holds him right away rocking him and talking to him. It's a beautiful moment for both of us. It's amazing how anything bad that has happened between us is instantly forgotten. It's only two minutes later after he hands Tyler over to me that his cell phone rings. Work is calling for him. He is running out the door just like that. I can't believe it. This is Nick stuck to a cell phone and business before anything else. I appreciate hard work, but leaving the hospital right after your son is born is pretty low. The doctors and nurses are totally surprised at this. I can tell they feel sympathy for me. Six hours later Nick does bring all of the kids to see us at the hospital. To me it doesn't make up for him leaving, but I am glad to see the kids here to welcome their new baby brother.

I am home the very next day. It doesn't take me long to get tired and feel those baby blues come on. I am on my own right away with all of the kids. Nick has to return to work. I am nursing every two hours. Tyler does not sleep much. And if he does sleep I am in full time mommy mode taking care of three little girls. My stitches are killing me. It's five o'clock. The girls are hungry for dinner. I break into tears and can't stop crying. I'm too tired. I feel really sad inside. I can't do this I think to myself. The girls see this and feel bad. They make themselves peanut butter and jelly. I'm grateful. I know this is a busy time for Nick with work, but I need some help. He is still coming home at all hours of the night. I would know because I am up at all hours of the night. My milk production is low. I am too tired and stressed. I am feeling severe depression at this point. I complain to Nick. He does not want my family here helping out. It's a long ride out to my parent's house and I don't want to stir up some aggravation with Nick and I don't want my parents to know how unhappy I am right now. I feel like a failure. Nick doesn't want me sharing our business with others.

Finally it's been a month and Nick is sending his sisters over to entertain the girls. I hire a sitter to take care of Tyler so I can get some much needed sleep. I take it upon myself to go pick her up. I make up some bottles ahead of time. I start up the van and start to back out of the garage not even realizing that the garage door is not all the way up. I am so tired. I start to back up and the top of the van hit the garage door. The tears just run down my face. The door and the back of the van are damaged. I don't want to tell Nick about this even though I know that he is going to find out. I decide to cancel the sitter and just stay put.

It is now evening. Nick's sisters are gone. The girls are chilled upstairs in their jammies. The van is in the garage with the garage door open. The garage door won't close all of the way. I'm totally fucked. He is going to kill me. He arrives in the driveway and walked straight to the garage. Oh God, I'm so scared right now. My stomach is in knots. I leave Tyler in his swing sleeping and walk over to the door that opens to our garage. He walks in furious. I look up at him in fear. His hand instantly goes to my neck and he is choking me against the wall screaming. "How dare you do this to me behind my back with my son in the car. You could have killed him!" He has this focus on my eyes telling me that he can kill me right now. "I'm sorry." I cry out. He lets me go. He grabs our son's car seat, packed the diaper bag, took the cell phones, all of the car keys, ripped the land line phone out of the wall, grabbed Tyler out of the swing and bolted out the door. I'm paralyzed. My son is gone. Oh my God. He just took my baby. How can I feed him? I fall to the floor hysterically crying. I don't know what to do besides wait for him to come back. I can't even call anyone. I don't have a phone. The next house is a long way down the road. What should I tell the girls. Thank God they have not run down here to see any of this. I wish I could tell Jennifer to come get Marley. Shit she can come get them all right now. I have no way to reach out for help. Why is he doing this to us? He is complete control.

It's ten a.m. the next day. I have been crying most of the night. I feel numb. I'm lying on the couch and I hear the footsteps of the girls. "Mommy, what's wrong?" Jessica asks as she kneels down next to me. I don't even know what to say. "I bet Nick was mean to her again" Julienne blurts out. "Where is Tyler?" Julienne is not stupid. She is used to seeing Tyler with me all of the time and knows that this is not normal. "Nick has him right now." I say "Mom, you can't feed him if Nick has him." She says. "I know." And then my tears start to fall again. "When is he coming back?" Marley asks. "I don't know." I say. "He is a bad man mom!" Julienne shouts. "Call my mom." Marley cries out. "I can't honey. Your dad took the phones and the keys to the cars." Jessica is so young and innocent and asks, "Is he just giving you a break so you can sleep now?"

It's an hour later and Nick comes in the door. Tyler is crying. Nick has a bottle with him so I know he tried to feed him. "What's the matter honey? Did you get the sleep that you needed?" I looked at him with hatred and grabbed my son out of his car seat. "I think he misses his mommy. What, did you think that I would hurt our son ro that I can't take care of him. I was trying to give you a break". "Where have you been with him? Why did you take the phones and the car keys? What if I or the girls needed medical help? What is wrong with you?" "Well, I didn't want you to have any interruptions. You needed to rest. Here is your phone and your keys. You don't need to call your friends and family over this. It will all be a misunderstanding of me trying to care for my wife. Oh and wait, it's my word against yours honey. Everything is fine now." He kisses my forehead. "I'm sorry for scaring you. I'm just very protective of our son. I will make this up to you. I have a sitter arranged and I'm taking you out for a romantic dinner tonight." I'm so emotionally drained. I just want to hold and feed my son and know that he is okay. I don't know what to say right now. I'm too tired to retaliate.

Nick did nothing but put me back on a pedestal and treat me with love and respect for the next couple months. We did things with the kids again. He bought me presents, sent me for massages, and had my car fixed and detailed. He was sorry. It must have been all of the stress building up from work. I forgave him.

THE CONTROL IS
TAKING OVER

ick is comfortable once again. We all seem to be very happy. Tyler is sleeping better at night. The kids are on a better sleeping schedule and Marley is back home at her mom's during the week so she can attend her own school. Marley missed her mother and friends so much. I finally worked on Nick enough to let her spend some time with her mom. Deep down I wanted the break too. I became the one to pick her up and take her home instead of Nick. Things go much smoother this way.

One day Marley was not ready to go yet. Jennifer looked like she just crawled out of bed and it was four o'clock in the afternoon. All the walls in her house were painted black and her drapes were all pulled closed. The house was very dark inside and dirty. It was so depressing to be in there. It was very odd and I felt a deep concern for both her and Marley. I did ask her how she was doing. "Well, ya know, we are trying to get by. Nick won't do his part so it's been tough." "Is he not paying your child support?" I ask. "Ha, Ha…No, and if he pays me anything it's not what he is supposed to pay me. If I fuck himI can get some cash out of him. Amy, I told you before to be aware. He makes sure we have nothing here, but he gives Marley the world over there. He abused me, cheated on me, and now controls me through our daughter. Just wait you will see." She calls for Marley. "Come on baby, Amy is waiting for you. She has to get going." I didn't know what to say after that. Marley came running down the hall and we headed out the door. "I will see what I can do about the child support. I will do what I can." I say as I walk away. "Thank you Amy."

We arrived at home and while I was making dinner I was trying to figure out how to approach Nick about the subject of child support. We live so comfortably and it appears that Marley and Jennifer live in poverty. I do not know what he pays her, but I have always assumed it was a fair amount. Would he really make his daughter suffer this way just to hurt Jennifer?

"Hi honey! I sold a big deal today!" as he rattles on and on about he pulled the rug out from under another new client. "And here is some cash for you to stash in our spot." as he winks at me. "A camper will be delivered tomorrow that was part of a trade for the unit I put in. This will be our new wheels up to the UP baby! It sure smells good in here. Where are my girls?" He yells as they come running down the stairs. "Dad is going to have a big surprise for you tomorrow!" "Yay", they say as they jump up and down. "What is it?" "You just have to wait and see." "Awww" they say as they all frown. "We want to know now." "Get ready for dinner that Mom has worked so hard on." They run back upstairs to wash their hands.

I just smile and adore everyone's happiness. Now is not the time to bring up the child support issue. It will have to be another time. We made crazy love that night. He was so passionate and told me how much he loved me. Life is good again.

ANOTHER TURN

hanksgiving is a week away and I would really like to spend it at my parent's house this year. We hardly ever see them. Nick always has a reason that we don't have time or can't make plans with them. They have only been out to visit a couple times. I stop in at the office with the kids to ask him about it. He suddenly has to make a phone call and ignores me knowing that I want something. He calls in coworkers and starts giving commands. When he is done he goes back to looking at his paperwork. "Nick!, hello do you not see us here? I want to talk to you about Thanksgiving." As I just stare at him in disbelief. "What!" He snapped. "Can we please have Thanksgiving with my family this year?" "No, I already told my mom we'd be with her." He said not even looking at me. "I have to get back to work. I will see you back at home later." What the fuck I thought. "Come on girls." I turned back around to look at him. "I'm not sure we will be home tonight." He looked up at me immediately with the eyes of I dare you and said, "Excuse me?" We walked out.

The kids and I go to McDonalds. My anger is brewing. I want to call my mom. I want to run back home. I can't do that. I can't make her worry. We eat, play, and head back home and settle in to watch a movie. Half way into the movie Nick storms in. "Amy, get in here. I need to talk to you." I suddenly feel my body go stiff and my stomach turn. I really pissed him off earlier. He grabs my arm as I walk into the kitchen and pulls me into the dining room. He pushes me back against the wall holding me at the chest with his right hand while pointing his left finger in my face. "Don't you ever talk back to me or threaten me like that again especially in front of my coworkers. If you want to stay in Tyler's life you better think twice about that bullshit. Do you hear me?" as he just stares me in the eyes. I'm paralyzed with fear and the tears are now running down my face. "Yes, I understand" I say with defeat. "Okay honey I am glad that we can agree on that." He now strokes my cheek lovingly, kisses me, and says he loves me. "God you are so beautiful. The UP has snow already. We are going on a snowmobile trip over the holiday with the kids. It will be a blast and we will bring a sitter to help with Tyler. It will be better than going to see our own families. Our family needs this." And before I can say a word he goes back into the living room to share the news with the kids.

UP VACATION

he camper is packed, the trailer is loaded with the snowmobiles, and the kids are excited. Maybe this will be a beautiful trip. It's a five-hour drive, but the kids will be able to move around in the camper and play on the way up there. We are driving in the evening hours so maybe they will even fall asleep at some point. We did have to wait for Nick to get off work to head out, but he seemed very jacked and ready to go.

The ride does end up being much longer than we expected. The snow is really coming down once we get into Wisconsin. We are driving pretty slow. I do notice some agitation coming from Nick while he is driving. He keeps drinking peppermint schnapps to keep him calm while he drives which I'm not a big fan of, but I'm afraid to aggravate him more by complaining about it. I was not hip on the rush to get up here tonight either. We could have waited until morning once we were all rested and refreshed. I was racing around like a nut case trying to pack up everything at record speed to have us on the road on time. Packing up for a whole family and food takes a lot of planning. I was feeling stressed myself before we even left. Thank God that we do have a sitter entertaining our children right now. I don't exactly have a lot of patience myself.

We are now eight hours into our drive and we hear a loud pop. Nick could feel the sudden drag and swaying of the trailer. "Shit!" He yells. "What's the matter?" I ask. "We just blew a tire on the trailer." We are not close to a gas station. "Do we have a spare?" I ask. "Fuck no we do not." I am thinking to myself how aggravated I have been with him since this whole thing started. Rushing to get on the road and now not being prepared properly with four little kids and a babysitter in hand. Nick is becoming more and more agitated. He hits the steering wheel as hard as he can. The only good thing about this is that the next gas station is right down the street. Nick gets out of the camper to go investigate the trailer. The tire blew, but he thinks we can get it down to the gas station. It's three o' clock in the morning. I just hope they are open. We will be sleeping in this camper if not. Nick is taking a while to come back. What is taking him so long to look at the trailer? When he finally does return he is suddenly full of energy and sniffing. His nose is really running and he keeps trying to clear his throat. I really do not want to believe what I am seeing. This is not happening again. God I hope that I am wrong.

The gas station was open and we were even able to get another tire. We arrive at our destination at four thirty in the morning. Everyone is asleep in the back. There is so much snow up here. It is beautiful. I wake the kids to go to get settled in our hotel rooms. We all need some rest. We all fall fast asleep. Well, everyone but Nick falls asleep. I woke to use the bathroom and he was not there. I am too tired to care at this point so I go back to sleep. About nine o'clock in the morning I hear Nick come into the room. He is taking off all of his snowmobile gear. He was out riding while we were sleeping. He has been up all night. Either he was just really excited to get out on those trails and filled with adrenaline or he is using again. I'm not going to let these thoughts ruin this trip for us.

We all make it outside after breakfast and its time to have some fun. All of us are in awe of how much snow that we see. The plows work around the clock up here. The kids and I stand next to the snow bank for a picture and the snow reaches way above our heads. We all run and jump in the snow. It's invigorating. Nick says, "See honey, aren't you glad we came?" with a smile on his face. "How about we let Tyler ride his little snowmobile around the parking lot while I get the other snowmobiles and the sleigh down off of the trailer?" Tyler was having a blast. He is so little and so cute. His ride could only go fifteen miles per hour max. This was the beginning of Tyler loving the UP just like his father.

We are all ready to ride. Our sitter retires back to the room. Nick is going to take her for a ride later after lunch. Nick, Tyler and I ride on his machine, while the girls are in tow in the sleigh in back of us. It's so funny to watch their three little helmets sway back and forth in unison as we glide down the trails. Over all we had so much fun. Tyler fell asleep riding in front of his dad.

Back at the resort we go down to the restaurant to eat. We are able to dance with and without the kids. We hold Tyler while we slow dance together. Nick has such a smile on his face and so much love in his eyes. I feel like I'm in heaven once again. Getting up here sucked, but I am seeing it was worth it. This is exactly what we need. Things will get back to normal. We just need a break and some quality family time.

VACATION OVER

All is happy back in our home. I am back to work again with Nick so that I can get out of the house. He is even training me on selling techniques. He tells me how good I will be at this. He is building my self-esteem which is really awesome for a change. He shares with me that he wants to expand the business, move to a larger building, and he will be needing my help. He is looking at a building here in town. "We could bring Tyler to work with us while the kids are in school. We could be together all of the time." He says to me while he runs his hands through my hair. It would be nice to be a part of something outside of the house and motherhood. Nick never wanted me to have a job as he felt there was no need for the money and I was needed more at home. What does he really want out of this though? What is changing his mind? Does he miss me that much? Does he really need my help like he says?

After months of hard work, the business is now officially in the new building. It's much bigger and everyone has their own private office now. We have a beautiful show room floor with a dedicated section to pools and spas. The other side has a nice professional showing of all of our water treatment units. Nick has asked me to use my expertise to sell the pools and spas along with the chemicals to treat them. Wow, he is making me part of something. I feel needed, important, and smart for a change.

Customers come in, listen to me, ask many questions, and I am able to answer them all. I feel good about myself. Nick will walk over at times and loves to introduce me to our customers with pride. This is great. I feel like a true part of the team. I work while the girls are in school, look after Tyler at work, and then get the girls from after school to go back home to my motherly duties and a house wife. Things are going quite smoothly for a while.

It's now been a few months into our new routine and I'm noticing a change in Nick's behavior. He is becoming more demanding of his staff including me. He is edgy and snapping at us. I'm now working into the evening hours having to bring the girls back to work with me after school. They now live on fast food for dinner. They do help me with Tyler. I set up the playroom so they can do their homework, watch movies, and do their best not to bother me. We are staying later and later on school nights. This is getting to be too much for all of us. Children need a routine with healthy environment to function, not to mention rest. Tyler is getting bigger and becoming more of a handful. Nick does take him on calls here and there to give me some relief, but his nap and meal times are all over the board. I'm exhausted and the kids are out of sync. This is not the life for them to be living.

It's nine o'clock at night. I need to get the kids home. They need their baths. They should already be in bed. The girls have school tomorrow. I try to track Nick down in the back of the store. I hear him yelling in Justin's office with the door closed. He is banging stuff around yelling at him. I can't understand what he is saying. Well, it's definitely not a good time to try to talk to him. I make the decision myself to pack up the kids and head home anyway. Enough is enough. I should not need his permission to leave for God's sakes.

As I am loading the kids in the van and getting Tyler buckled into his car seat, here comes Nick. He does not look happy. "Where do you think you are going?" "Nick, I need to get the kids home. It's late. We are all tired. The girls have school tomorrow." "There is still work to do Amy! The business is struggling. This new building comes with a lot more expenses." He says to me with his arm over the top of the car and blocking me from being able to move. "Come on Nick. Seriously, the kids come first. It's nine o' clock. We have been here all day." "Fine, Go!" He yells. Geez I think to myself. I get into the driver's seat, close my door, start the engine, and start to back up. He slams his hand on the hood of the car and just stares at me with evil in his eyes. I and the kids are scared. They say nothing. I notice Julienne is starting to cry quietly.

The kids are settled in. I'm physically exhausted, but on edge afraid of what is to come next. I feel the need to be on guard. I can't sleep. What is going to happen when he comes home? When is he going to come home? My stomach feels sick. I'm worried about my kids. Maybe nothing will happen. He just needs to calm down, see things from my point of view, and he will apologize. I doze off in and out of sleep. I turn to look at the clock. It's two in the morning. He is not here in bed. I decide to go downstairs to look around and see if his car is in the garage. Nope, it's not here. Where is he? I feel somewhat relieved because I do not want to deal with him out of fear, but at the same time I feel so hurt about the way that he is treating me. Am I being punished? I just don't understand what is going on. What did I do wrong? The tears fall and my body just shakes. I'm feeling so isolated again. Do I show up at the store tomorrow? I'm afraid not to. There will be other employees there so what can he do to me? Maybe that is a good place to be when I do see him again. The night continues on. He does not come home. I do not sleep. It's time to start a new day.

I can tell the girls are tired this morning. They are crabby and picking on each other. I had a really hard time waking Julienne. Tyler is still sleeping which is unusual. I'm totally out of sorts and I know that the girls can sense it. I get Julienne on the bus. Jessica is ready for preschool. I get in the shower and make myself presentable before I get Tyler out of bed. Once I get him up he is so fussy. He doesn't want to eat his breakfast. He will only accept a bottle to calm him. We head out, I drop Jessica at her school, and Tyler and I make it to the store. Nick's jeep is here. Well, here we go.

He is in his office. I take Tyler into the play room and get him comfortable in his playpen. I sit with him watching for customers to come in. Nick hears me. He walks in and picks up Tyler. "How's my boy?" He kisses him and carries him out the door. He did not look at me or say hello to me. My heart sinks. I want to leave. I feel hate towards him. Why is he doing this to me? He looks like shit. Did he even sleep last night? It sounds like he is coming down with a cold. He suddenly comes back in the playroom and asks, "Where is his diaper bag?"" Right here. "I say as I hand it to him. "Want to work with your daddy today? We have to go to the bank first and get some money. Everyone needs to get paid." Why is he saying all of this? What's wrong with just writing everyone a paycheck. Next thing I know they are out the door. I just sit here for a moment in a daze. I cry not knowing what to do next.

THE TRUTH
COMES OUT

ustin walks in after he knew Nick was gone looking at me with sympathy in his eyes. "It has started hasn't it?" he asks me. I look at him in confusion. "What do you mean?" "The abuse. The abuse that Jennifer went through." The tears just flood from my eyes as he holds me tight. "He is using again Amy." "Using what?" "You are so innocent and naïve if you don't know. Cocaine. The company is going bankrupt because of his habit. He is spending a lot of money on it and he is not selling because of it. His behavior is becoming erratic. He relapsed a while back and it is now out of control. You and the kids are in danger. It only gets worse from here. You need to start making plans to get out. Do not tell him that

I told you this." I just looked at him in shock. My head is spinning. I am so scared. "What are you and the other employees going to do?" I ask. "Don't worry about us. Plans are in the making. We all know where this is going. Contact your family for help. In the meantime Brian or I can stop in regularly to check in on you. We will make an excuse. He has Tyler." I cry even more. "I don't know what to do." "Go home and get the kids things together like birth certificates, any cash lying around, a bag of clothes, and be ready to call the police and go into hiding. You are being abused by an addict. The police tend to be on the Richardson side around here because of business flow in a small town. Be prepared to escape. You will see Tyler again. It's his way to mess with you. And do not drive the Ford Escort company car. He has been known to stash drugs in it somewhere and I'd hate to see you get caught with it."

As I'm driving back to the house thoughts are racing through my head. It makes sense now why Nick and I had visited a few banks one day. He had a brief case and would return to the car with cash in it. We would get back to the office and he called everyone in to get paid. I heard arguing that they weren't getting paid their full pay. And why were they not getting a pay check anymore? I get home and get stuff put together for all of us and hide it in the basement. I can't believe I am doing this. Do I call the police now? I can't prove anything. It's his word against mine. He has Tyler still. I have to play stupid. I don't want to call my parents just yet. Next thing I know the phone rings. I answer. "Hello." "Hi honey! I'm here with some customers that would love to meet you and want you to show them how to care for their spa. They are having some trouble. Come on over and bring some samples and coupons." He gives me the address. I'm not going to say no and he knows it because he has Tyler. "Okay, I'll be there in fifteen minutes or so." I say as nice as I can.

When I arrive I put on my fake smile and personality and do as he asks. He hands Tyler over, thanks me, and says that he'll see us later tonight with a kiss on my forehead. Sick bastard I think to myself.

Tyler is fussy in the car on the way home and I feel the need to go grab Jessica from preschool. It's about lunch time. I pick her up early. She is so happy to see me. She gets out of naptime today even though she falls asleep on the way home. My poor babies is all that I can think about right now.

We are home and I make some lunch. Jessica finishes up and heads upstairs to play with her Barbie's. Tyler is finger painting with his food in his high chair. Well at least he is content. The door knocks and to my surprise one of Nick's longtime friend and employee walks in the door. "Well Hello." I said. "How are you?" "Good, I'm checking in on you." He says. "I know things are getting a little crazy. I wanted to make sure you guys are okay." How kind I thought. I asked him if he wanted some lunch but he declined.

Not even two minutes later I hear screeching tires in the driveway and then a slamming car door. Nick storms in the house screaming. "What the fuck are you doing here? Are you fucking my wife behind my back?" He is charging towards me with rage in his eyes. I grab my keys on the counter. "Brian watch the kids!" I run out the front door and head for my car. I'm in my car and I start the engine with the doors locked. He runs behind me, smashes my side mirror, and beats on the windshield causing it to crack. He is screaming at me at the top of his lungs to open the car door. I'm shaking, but I get the car in reverse to get away. I speed down the country roads. He catches up to me and literally tries to run me off the road. We approach a couple on a motorcycle as we are entering town that I almost hit and finally he backs off. I head straight to the police station while the couple follows me. Nick has disappeared. He knew exactly where I was headed.

I'm in the police station parking lot. The couple runs up to me. "Are you okay honey?" they ask. I'm trembling. I can't talk. I'm alive. I could have been killed. I can't move. She stays with me while he runs in to get the police. They are my witnesses. The police run out. I manage to get out of the car. The couple gives their statement and I manage to finally tell what had just happened. "Oh my God! My children. They are still at home!" "We will send an officer now to your house." She is female. She appears nice. She knows who Nick is. She went to school with him. "It sounds like Nick is under a lot of stress. Is there any where you can go and stay while he cools off?" I look at her in disbelief. "What? Shouldn't he be arrested? I want an order of protection. "We can pick him up and hold him overnight. He can get out until a court date is set. In the mean time we suggest that you find another place to stay or we can direct you to a shelter for abused women in Rockford for you and your children where you will be safe. You can request and file an order of protection and be seen in front of the judge as early as tomorrow. We do still need to find Mr. Richardson. We will be with you at your home while you gather your things so he can't get to you." All the while I am thinking to myself why do I have to leave and turn my kid's life upside down because of what he did?

I make it back to the house. Brian and the police are here waiting for me. Brian offers to have me stay with him at his place for the night with the kids so I can calm down and figure things out. He says that he will protect us. I do not want to go to the shelter so I agree. I get our things together. Jessica is crying with fear and confusion in her eyes. I take the kids with me to grab Julienne from school. My paperwork is already filed and I have to be in court at nine o'clock tomorrow morning. I can't bring the kids to court. I will bring them to school tomorrow and make sure the school is aware of the situation and that Nick is not to go near them. Brian is going to have to go with me tomorrow and look after Tyler in the lobby. What a mess this is. It is time to call my parents and let them know what is going on. I will call them tomorrow when everything including me calms down. I have done all that I can for the time being. We are safe.

It takes me a while to calm the girls and reassure them that everything is going to work itself out. They have me and we are going to figure everything out tomorrow after a good night's sleep. We snuggle together on the floor as they drift off to sleep. Tyler and I head up onto the bed, snuggle, and watch T.V. He still has his bottle. He is getting too old for it, but the way things are right now I need every vice that I can get my hands on. It is not the time to worry about yanking his bottle away. He zonks out in record time. I am mentally drained and zonk out shortly after him.

It's still dark and I awake to pounding and yelling. I listen harder trying to understand what the yelling is about.

It's Nick and Brian arguing. Brian says, "Nick you need to leave now! I'm going to call the police!" He reacts back. "I knew it! You are fucking my wife. Her car is here. Let me in damn it!" "Nick you are wired on coke. Get out of here man before you do something stupid. You are my friend, I love you, but you fucking need help! Leave them alone. You have your family scared to death of you. You are throwing your family and your business away over what? You are a junkie." "Oh, you are one to talk. Who bailed your ass out during your binges big man?" "That was a long time ago man." "What the fuck. Now you are taking my family" Nick you are out of your mind." Brian finally says. I get up and come out of my room. I look at Nick with serious eyes of hatred. "I'm calling the police Nick. Stay the fuck away from us!" And then he fled. I did call the police and hoped that they caught up with him. This is all the more reason to be granted this order of protection. I need to check into the shelter first thing after that and go from there. God I hate to do this.

OFF TO THE SHELTER

he temporary order of protection is granted. It's good for two weeks at which I will have to come back to court if I want it to stick permanently. He can't come near me or the kids. He has no access to their school or daycare. We have the option to stay in our home. I am questioning if that is a safe decision. He's already out of his mind. Maybe we should just go to the shelter for a day or two until things calm down. I have no idea how he is going to react once he gets served and it's probably best that he does not know where we are at. If I were to go to my parent's house it would be so crowded and the kids would have to change schools. They need to keep some kind of stability through this. Being around structure and their friends is something they need. I think we would all be uncomfortable living under my parent's roof. The shelter can lead us to some other options hopefully.

"Thank you Brian for everything." I say as I grab Tyler from him in the lobby. "I need to get over to the shelter now and figure out what to do next." "No problem. My door is always open. I'm sorry that you are going through this. It's not fair to you and these kids. I really hope he gets the help that he needs before shit hits the fan. Things are about to get really ugly and you should start looking for work for back up." He says to me with sympathy in his eyes.

I'm in downtown Rockford in front of the building. It does not have any signs. It's old and painted with brown brick in between two other old office buildings. There is only parallel parking here. It's quite gloomy and scary.

I park my van, grab Tyler out of his car seat, and look around to make sure that I'm not being watched or followed. I get up to the door of the address that they gave me. I see that I have to be buzzed in. I push the button. "Can I help you?" I explain that I have been sent by the Rochelle police and now have an order of protection in hand on my husband. "I will buzz you in and a social worker will come down to greet you." "Okay." I say hesitantly.

I walk into a small room with a couple glass windows. The door to the next hallway is locked. This must be part of the protection process for the residents here. I hear footsteps coming down the stairs and then I see an African American woman through the glass coming to the door. "Hello hon. My name is Ruth. Please come on in. What an adorable boy you have there." I smile and say "Hi. And thank you." We will head upstairs so you can meet one of our caseworkers and give us all of your information. Let's see what we can do to help."

I am already in the computer system. I am told all of the rules of the shelter and what my responsibilities are while residing here. Now I am given my tour. There are rows of rooms with bunk beds. I find out that we will not have our own rooms and will have to share with others. These rooms are really small. Curfew to be back in the building if we leave is nine p.m. Lights go out at ten p.m. There is a large common area with a television and toys for the kids to play with. There is another open room next to it with long cafeteria tables and a huge kitchen. All of the moms cook and clean on rotating schedules. There is a payphone for our use in the hallway. There are only three bathrooms for all of us to share. There is a bulletin board in the hallway full of job postings and classes at the local colleges. All I can think is I feel like I'm going to jail. How is this fair? Why is my life so upside down and uncomfortable? My eyes start to water and stomach is in knots I'm not sure that I can do this.

"Here is the room that you and your children will be sleeping in. Your girls will get these two bunk beds while you and your son share this lower bunk over here. Latina and her two children get the other three beds. Beds are to be made and clothes neatly put away every morning. Everyone is out of bed no later than seven in the morning. Breakfast will be served at 7:45 sharp. There is a rotation schedule for shower use for each family in the am or pm each day. If you are not working, going to court, or have any appointments to attend to we have group therapy at 11:00 right before lunch. If you leave, you must sign out and back in and also know what your plans are for the day. This is so we can know that you are safe and accounted for. I'll let you get settled in and come back to take you to meet some of the other moms." Ruth gives me a small smile and turns away to her business.

I need compassion right now. I need to fall into someone's arms and cry my eyes out. I haven't done anything wrong. I'm just trying to protect us. I feel like I'm in jail. Tyler is so fussy right now. He won't settle in my arms. Do I let him move around freely? Am I allowed to do that? My daughters are going to hate this place. What if Tyler won't settle at night and keeps everyone awake. He is used to his own room and his crib. The tears keep falling. I need to know when Nick is served and how he reacts. We can try this for a day or two, but I'm not so sure that this is going to work for us.

I am now taken to meet the other moms. There are only six women in the room right now. Two women are sitting on the couch watching television with infants in their arms. The other four are chasing around their toddlers and yapping away with each other. Only one woman is white. They are talking in a slang language. You can tell that they are from the rough parts of town. They probably think this place is luxury. How in the world am I going to fit in here?

"Girls, this is Amy and her son Tyler. Please welcome her and introduce yourselves. Ruth basically orders them to do so. A couple of the women turn to look at me and just stare me down. I could read their minds. I know that I don't belong here in their territory. I instantly do not feel well in their presence. "Hello Sugar." One of them says walking towards me. She stops and puts her hands on her hips. "Welcome to the club. I am Leandra and this is my son Calvin. He still has a black eye from his daddy. Second time we here." She then turns and walks away while the others look up at me and then right back to what they are doing.

What do I do next? I have to pick up the girls in two hours. We will not be staying here long at all. I need to put a plan together. I take Tyler back to our room and try to get him to nap for a bit while I cry some more.

I get the girls with no hassles and no signs of Nick. I take them to McDonalds with a play place in Rockford for an early dinner so that they all can get some energy out and do their homework here. I now have to break the news to them of where we will be staying tonight. "Can't we stay somewhere else. Why isn't Nick in jail? I want to sleep in my own bed mom." Julienne says in aggravation. "It's okay mom. As long as we are all together we are going to be okay. I'll help you take care of Tyler." Jessica says to me while she gives me a big hug. I have such wonderful children. Julienne is so angry and how can I blame her. "Guys, it's just for a night or two to figure out what we should do next okay?" I say with hopeful acceptance in my eyes. "Let's go pick up some of your favorite snacks, a couple of favorite books to read, some of those crafty necklaces that you like to make, and a couple of toys to keep Tyler busy and relaxed to pass some of the time." I don't have a lot of money. I should have taken that cash out of our spot at home, but I was too afraid of what Nick would do. I have my own checking account still so I have some control of my own money. I am down to $950.00. I am so tired and emotionally drained. I have no appetite. I have to keep it together for my kids.

We arrive back at the shelter and get settled into our room before the other family is in there with us. We are all on edge and very uncomfortable. "This is where we have to sleep?" Julienne asks. "Yes." I say as my eyes start to tear up again. She knows not to say anymore. She takes care of her sister which I believe is comforting her.

Latina has one girl that is six years old and one boy that is four years old. They are not mean to us when they walk in, but they are not exactly friendly either. "Does your little guy sleep well at night?" she asks. I can tell she is concerned about him keeping everyone up at night. I am too for that matter. "Well, being here and not in his own bed I hope that he does okay. I apologize ahead of time if he is a problem. I will sit in the common area if I have to." I reply. She nods her head and says, "Good, I am glad that we have this understanding. My babies need their sleep. They attend school." "I understand, mine do too." I go to get milk for Tyler's bottle and tell the girls that it is time for bed. They obeyed and thank God all of the kids slept through the night. I on the other hand tossed and turned. I prayed that Julienne would not wet the bed due to all of the stress. Damn, I forgot to buy pull ups for her.

It's morning. It's so loud. My watch says that it's only six in the morning. I hear babies crying and toddlers screeching. Mommas are yelling at their children to not fight and to wait their turn for the bathroom. Pots and pans are clanking and the pouring of cereal and milk is present. It sounds like a zoo in this place. I'm getting my kids freshened up and going to get us breakfast elsewhere. I can't do this.

TIME TO TURN
TO A FRIEND

get the girls back off to school and head over to Carol's. I hate to put her on the spot. She just had a baby, but I really need her help right now.

"Oh Amy, of course you guys can stay here for a bit." She says. She holds me tight, I tremble and just break down. "I'm so tired and I just don't know what to do. I want to go home, but I'm afraid. He needs help to get off the drugs. He's crazy. I'm probably going to have to live with my parents. I can't manage on my own. I don't have the skills to make a decent living. Nick is going bankrupt. I will go crazy living with my parents." I cry out. "Let's go get you set up downstairs. Then we will call the police station to see if Nick has been served. If so, Arthur will go with you to your house to grab more of your things tonight. We are going to put your car in the garage right now. Go take a hot shower and I'll grab ya a glass of wine. You need to relax and chill for a while. I am so grateful for her right now. I do need to slow down and breathe. "I can watch over Tyler. Go on."

Nick did get served last night at the shop. Arthur took me over to my house. Nick was not home so I grabbed stuff quickly for the kids and I. I'm a nervous wreck. I can't think fast enough. I'm afraid to run into him again. Within ten minutes I had what I needed. I did look for the cash, but it was gone. I watch for his car to make sure that we are not being watched or followed. I just want some peace tonight. The kids and I just need to relax and feel safe. I have no idea what to do from here. If anything maybe this will be a wakeup call for Nick to go get some help.

Carol brings down popcorn and juice boxes for the kids. She makes sure that we have plenty of blankets and towels. The kids are much more content now that we are no longer at that shelter. They are actually laughing and being silly. "Okay guys. In a half hour it's lights out. Carol and the new baby need things to be quiet around here. They need their rest. It's 8:30 at night and I know that Carol is exhausted. She has not had a nap all day and is nursing every two to three hours. I feel so bad about the timing of this, but I just don't know where else to turn at the moment.

Julienne looks down at her hands while she fidgets with them and then asks me, "Mom when do we get to go back home?" I don't know what to say to her. I don't know from one hour to the next what we are going to do from here. I do not know how to put a plan together. Right now I am just so damn tired. "I'm not sure yet sweetie." She blows out steam in her frustration and then just turns to ly down. Jessica comes over to me and gives me a big hug. She knows that I am falling apart. "Tyler needs his bottle." I say. "He will never settle down without it." "I'll get it mommy; you rest." She says.

It's ten thirty at night and the house is dark and quiet. Everyone is sleeping and I am finally feeling somewhat relaxed. I'm sleepy. My body is giving in. My legs and arms start to twitch as they relax. I drift off to sleep. It's still dark and I'm not sure what time it is, but I awaken by Carol's dogs barking upstairs by the front door. I look up and she is there at the door. "It's him isn't it?" I ask

She looks so tired and aggravated. She nods her head yes. She starts to open the door and I say "No wait, let me handle this. Go back to bed. This is not your problem." I could tell that she was relieved, but the dogs would not stop barking which in turned woke the baby. Carol is annoyed and cranky. I feel bad. I know that I need to call the police, but I also want to put this fire out quietly and calmly for their sake. I knew that he would find me here even with my car in the garage.

I open the door and step outside. Nick is crying. "Nick what are you doing here? It's the middle of the night. I have a restraining order against you. "Please." He cries to me. "I am not here to hurt you. I am so sorry. I love you so much. I do not want you and our kids to have to live like this. They need their home and their own beds. You look so tired honey. You need to be back in your own home so you can rest. Just let me take care of you guys the way that I used to. No more drugs. I saw my sponsor tonight. I'm back at meetings. I will get things back on track. Just give me a chance. I can't live without you. Look me in the eyes and tell me that you don't love me anymore. I know that you feel the way that I do deep down in your gut. Nobody has what we do. I never knew what it was to make true love to somebody until I met you.

I look him in the eyes and my tears start to fall. He's right. I do love him. I want all of this to be over. I am exhausted. I want to go home. "No more drugs?" I ask "Nope, no more." He says with a smile of hope on his face. "I'll see you back at home tomorrow after I get the girls off to school." I say. And that is all it took. He charmed me, I believed him, and I went back.

WE ARE BACK HOME

t feels good to be back in my home. Nick is showering me with all of the love and attention that anyone could ask for. He has not been overbearing or mentally abusive in any way towards me or the girls. He gives them their space. While the girls are in school during the day he takes Tyler and I with him on his errands, sales calls, lunch, etc.

Today is a different day. Tyler seems warm when I dress him and his eyes are all glassy. He is irritable and does not even want his bottle. He must not be feeling well. Nick walks into the bedroom. "Nick, Tyler and I are going to stay home today. He is coming down with something." I say to him. He picks up Tyler, kisses him on his cheek and says, "You are a Richardson and a daddy's boy. You will be fine. Tell your momma that she worries too much. "He says to Tyler. "Honey come on and get him ready. He will be fine. It's probably just a little cold." "But what is the big deal if we just stay here so he can rest. He does not need to be dragged all over town." I point out to him. Nick is becoming agitated. I can tell by the way he puts his hands on his hips, lifts his chin, comes close to me, and stares me down with his eyes. I do not like what I am feeling at this very moment. I do not say another word. I do not want to strike another nerve. His body language is bringing back some bad memories. "Fine!" he says. "You are right. I will be by to check in on you guys later. I'll bring back some lunch for you. Now he strokes my cheek and winks at me. He keeps his cool. He knows that he has to. This is the first day in weeks that we will not be spending a lot of the day together. Or maybe he doesn't trust me. He can't stand to spend any time away from me. He kisses both Tyler and I on the forehead and heads to work.

I give Tyler some Tylenol and then we go snuggle on the couch to watch some of his favorite cartoons As he starts to doze off I can hear the stuffiness in his nose. "Yep buddy, good thing that we are staying home. You are getting a bug for sure. I am starting to doze back off myself when I hear the phone ring. I look at the clock. Nick just left forty-five minutes ago. I do not want to move Tyler to pick up the phone. I just got him back to sleep. I ignore the call and let it go to the answering machine. The answering machine is in the other room so I can't hear it. I have a cell phone, but it's upstairs. I hope that it's nothing important. I'll check the message in a little bit. Two minutes later the phone rings again. Oh come on, seriously I think to myself. Shit I better get up to answer it. It could be the school calling. I slide out from under Tyler as carefully as I can. He stirs and whimpers, but stays asleep. I walk across the living room and answer the phone. "Hello." I say. "What the hell Amy? Why didn't you answer the first time that I called." Nick asks me. Are you fucking kidding me is all I can ask myself. I explain to him the situation and why I did not want to get up to get the phone. "I need you to come into the office right now and help me." "Nick Tyler has a fever. He is sick. I need to be here at home with our son right now! He is sleeping. Why are you being like this?"" He can sleep in the car. I need you here with me right now." He says. You have got to be fucking kidding me I think. He can't go one day with me being with him at his side. "No Nick. I'm staying right here! Maybe later." He slams down the phone. God, what is his problem?

Tyler wakes up an hour later. The sleep and Tylenol is working it's wonder. He gets up, walks into the kitchen, and points to the fridge. He is hungry now. As I am pulling out a Gogurt Nick bolts through the door. He is so angry. "You need to stand by me Amy so our employees know that everything is going to be okay!" He shouts at me. He gets in my face and orders me to pack up Tyler's things and get ready to head back out with him. "You need to help at the shop!" He yells. His eyes are threatening and his body is hovering over me. I'm arching backwards. I can't stand the heat of his breath on my face. I feel fear and just give in to what he wants. "Fine." I say.

I get home late with all of the kids just like before and Tyler's fever spikes late in the evening. I'm up all night with a miserable toddler. In the morning I do take Tyler to the doctor to confirm that he has yet another inner ear infection. I am not going to fight with Nick, but I will refuse come hell or high water to go in to help him today. I'm staying home with Tyler period. I am once again asking myself how am I ever going to be healthy, happy, or even at least a good mother living under the same roof with him? Even if he is no longer using drugs which I am starting to question he is who he is period. He may not be physically abusing me at the moment, but he is doing a damn good job of mentally abusing me. He is not going to change. I am once again feeling unsafe and anxious. I want to cry. It's time to call my parents this time for real. I have to get us out of here.

I did get to stay home with Tyler all day yesterday after all. Nick did not return back home until midnight. This is a bad sign that he is using again. I roll over in bed to look at the clock. It's only five thirty in the morning. The sun has not even shown through the window yet. Nick is rolled over on his side sound asleep. It smells like booze in here. Just great I think. I try to get comfortable and fall back to sleep for a while. I awaken Nick and he rolls over next to me. He instantly starts fingering me while his rock hard penis is rubbing up against my leg. I really don't want to do this right now, but if I give him what he wants he will probably get over his pathetic behavior and be nice to me again. Within seconds he gets up on his knees and flips me up on to mine. He penetrates me fucking me hard and fast. When he is finished he slaps my ass and asks, "How was that honey?" Have you missed me? I wanted to start your day out right." He chuckles with pride. "Time to get up and get ourselves ready for work." He says as he coughs and sniffles. "I'll make some bacon and eggs for everyone." He says. He knows that the girls hate eggs. He has forced them to eat them in the past to the point of making them gag, cry, and not be able to leave the table.

The girls go to school in tears because of the eggs. Now I'm upset too. I give Tyler his medicine while I hold back my tears. This has got to stop. I follow Nick's orders today and we go to work together. We are at the shop for about an hour and a call comes in for service. Nick wants to take it. It's a possible sale for new equipment. Tyler and I stay at the shop because somebody needs to watch the floor. Bingo, this is my chance to call my mom and tell her what is going on.

HELLO MOM

"Hi Mom, how are you?" I ask after she answers the phone. "We are all pretty good. How are you guys? We have not heard from you in a long time. I have left you a couple messages to give us a call." She replies. I hesitate for a moment. I'm so afraid Nick will walk into that door at any minute. "I don't have a lot of time to talk Mom. The kids and I are in trouble. It's Nick. He is the reason that you don't hear from me or see us. "I blurt this out as fast as I can. "I was afraid of this. Has he physically hurt any of you?" "Yes." I say while my voice trembles. I can't hold the tears back. I'm finally telling her what is going on. "We need to get all of you out of there Amy." She tells me outright. "Oh shit, Nick is here I have to go. I will call back when I can." I hang up the phone and quickly focus my attention on the shelf that I start to clean.

My eyes are swollen. He is going to want to know why. At least my parents know what is going on now. There is no turning back from that. They are going to get involved and It is not going to be pretty.

"Hi Amy. Hey buddy. Daddy just sold another one! Whew hoo!" Nick says while he does his little dance in front of Tyler. Hi Amy, I think to myself. He said it so cold too. What is that about? "Amy I am sending you with the company card to Farm and Fleet to pick up some parts for this job. I'll write it all down for the sales guy. Tyler will stay here with me, right buddy? Who's my boy?" He basically just ordered me. I did not get a please or a thank you. He just turns away and walks back to the back of the shop with Tyler to talk to the guys. He knows that I have been crying. It's not like I can hide it. He didn't ask me why. Should I be relieved or hurt that he doesn't even care that I am upset about something? This is so twisted in my mind. I want to scream at him and yell "NO!". I can't do it. I do not want any repercussions from my retaliation. It's not worth it.

I get to Blain's Farm and Fleet. I'm walking in the front doors and look to my right. Well look at this. Now is my chance to call my mom back. I can call my mom back collect on this payphone. I make the call and explain that I have to keep the conversation quick. I tell her about everything that has been happening. "We are going to meet all of you for a birthday lunch to see the kids and give you presents. Do not bring Nick. We are going to use this as an excuse so that he won't question what you are doing. Have your bags packed. You will not be coming back. Can you pull this off?" She asks me. "I will do my best. When?" "We can meet you at the buffet in Rockford tomorrow at noon.

It's Saturday so the kids are not in school. Has Nick made any plans for you guys as of yet?" "No, but that can change in a heartbeat with him." I reply. "Wait until tomorrow morning to tell him unless he leaves for work. Don't even bother to tell him then."

I get the list of things that he wants as quickly as I can. I walk back to the car a nervous wreck. I have to calm down and act normal. My stomach is starting to twist and I feel nauseated. My hands are shaking. God why am I going through this? What did I do to deserve this?

I walk into the shop and the first thing that I hear is Tyler crying. I know that he is still not feeling well. I want to take him home now! I walk into Nick's office. He is not in here. Tyler is here standing in his playpen crying. His eyes are swollen and tired. He has yellow snot all over his face. I pick him up, put on his jacket, and leave. This is ridiculous. As I am driving home my cell phone rings. I know that it's him. I do not want to answer it, but I do. "Amy, where are you going with my son?" he asks in an aggravated voice. "I can't do this job unless you are here!" "Nick!" I finally yell. "I am taking our son home! He is miserable. He needs rest and to be comforted right now. Ask one of your guys or secretary to watch the floor!" I can't believe that I yelled at him that way. God only knows what is going to happen to me now. At least my parents are informed of the situation now. He slams down the phone and I continue driving home.

I am home. Amazingly Nick has not called or come to the house. I left with Tyler three hours ago. Tyler has been peacefully sleeping two of those hours. Julienne will be getting off the bus soon and then we have to head out to pick up Jessica. I go back to their rooms to pack some of their things in a suitcase. I need to hide it somewhere. I hide it way in the back of Julienne's closet. I decide to do the same with Tyler's stuff. I go to my bedroom and pack my things along with all important paperwork and some cash from our dresser drawer. Well, I'm ready. Everything is packed. I am not going to say anything to the girls. We are just going to go. I'll get their suitcases in the back of the car in the morning so they won't suspect anything.

Nick is out all night once again. I look at the clock and it's seven am. He is not here. This is fine with me. I get the girls up just like any other day. I'll tell them that I have a surprise for them to get them to move quickly. We need to get out of here as quickly as possible. "Hurry up and get ready girls." I say in a happy motivated voice. I do everything that I can to not show them any fear. While they are in the bathroom brushing their teeth and hair, I grab all out our stuff and get it into the back of the car. Tyler was still in his crib so I was able to act fast. I go up to get Tyler. He is standing up in his crib patiently waiting for me. I made sure to bring up a bottle for him while I get him changed and ready to go. I showered last night so I only had to do a quick freshen up. We hurry down to the car, kids all get buckled in safe, and we are out of there.

Whew, we did it! I head to the Rockford area and make sure to let my mom know that we are headed that way on my cell phone. It's early, but we had to go when we had the chance. "Where are we going Mom?" Julienne asks. It is at this point that I find a parking lot to pull into. I tell my girls what is going on. "I knew it." Julienne says as she rolls her eyes. I keep them busy until lunch time. We go to McDonalds and then to the park so the kids can run around and play for a while. We still have an hour to kill before we meet my parents for lunch so we head over to Walmart to buy a couple toys and some things to keep them busy at the restaurant while my parents and I talk.

We pull into the parking lot of the buffet and my parents are there in the parking lot waiting. They see us and get out of the car. I roll down my window to see what they want to do. "Does Nick know that we are here?" my mom asks. "No he never came home last night and honestly I'm quite surprised that he hasn't called my cell phone yet." "Okay good. Dad is going to drive your van and you and the kids are going to get in my car and ride with me. He will be looking for your van. I want all of us to get out of here safely and quickly. We can sit down and eat somewhere farther from here. We are going to take a little trip up to the Dells to be out of site from him and get some kind of a plan put together. You are with us and you are safe now." I break into tears and step out of the van. She grabs me in her arms and holds me. For once I feel that I can let my guard down. "Turn off your phone now. We don't need him upsetting you anymore. We all know that he is going to try to reach out to you and will probably be out of his mind." I do as she says and off we go.

LIVING WITH THE P'S

oing to Wisconsin Dells was good for all of us to wind down and get our thoughts together. But we are now back at my parent's house getting settled in to our new home. The first week was okay, but now we are all getting on each other's nerves. It's never easy to go back home when you are used to living your own life. I knew this would happen. This is why I waited so long to reach out to them. The girls are sharing a bed in the basement, while Tyler and I take a room upstairs. I feel so much anger that my life has been turned upside down.

My parents find me a lawyer and a huge retainer fee. $5000.00 is a lot of money for them. It must be all of their savings. My mom and I later went to apply for help for the kids and I. I qualify for food stamps, Medicaid, and daycare so I can go find a job. I enroll the girls in their new school out here. They are not fond of any of this. I can't blame them. All of these changes are too much for anyone to take let alone a child.

My first job is in a factory working nights. I pick out damaged plastic medical pieces from one box to another. I can hardly stay awake. The work is so boring and monotonous. I just can't do this. I later get a job working for a maid service. It's not too bad. It is hard physical work for sure. They pay is low, but it's a job. I'm becoming so depressed. I am not comfortable living in my parent's house. I need my own place, but I can't afford it. I have not received any child support yet. Everything should be worked out in court in another week. I was able to get another order of protection. Nick has not come here, so he must have been served. I don't think that he wants to mess with my parents.

Our court date is here. Both of my parents go with me to Rochelle. I am so nervous about seeing Nick again. Tyler is with a sitter and the girls are in school. We walk through security and wait in the common area upstairs. God I hate this place. It's such a small town and everyone knows of someone who is there. I hear Nick's voice talking as he is walking up the stairs. He is on his cell phone as usual. We lock eyes. A chill runs down my spine and my gut is turning. It sounds like he is talking to another girl about what a nice time that had together last night. Another one of his mind fucks to get to me of course. God he is good. I'll give him that much. I can't believe I care enough to feel jealous and hurt.

Our names are called and we all head into the court room. Nick takes advantage to open his mouth real quick. "You doing okay Amy? You look tired. How is our son?" My mom instantly grabs me into a quick embrace and tells me to ignore him and keep walking to our seats. We settle into the benches. Nick is on one side of the courtroom while we are on the other. When our case is called we stand in front of the judge with our attorneys. They do all of the talking for us of course. Child support is set and he is actually going to get visitation rights. We have to meet at a police station to exchange him every other weekend. My divorce is under way.

AND SO IT BEGINS

ur court dates continue. Nick does not pay his child support. He claims that his business is in financial trouble. The judge orders him to catch it up anyway seeing that he only has to pay fifty dollars per week. Hell, what am I supposed to do with that? He is such an asshole and full of shit. If he doesn't catch up his support money today there will be an order out for his arrest.

It's been one month later and our divorce is finalized. Our exchanges with Tyler are getting harder and harder for me. I do take Tyler by myself now since I feel safe at the police station. My parents have enough of their own things to worry about. This time he is civil to me. He brings his girlfriend with him. I know this is to hurt me. Why does this hurt me so much? I feel sadness. Even after everything that he has done to the kids and I, I realize that

I still miss him. How sick can this be? What is wrong with me? I miss him and still love him. I feel this urge to talk to him once again.

"Everything okay Amy?" He sees my eyes watering while I'm trying to hold back my emotions. He looks handsome and I can smell his Eternity cologne. Why does he do this to me? Why can't I let go after everything that has happened? When he gets the chance he says quietly, "I miss you too. I am sorry for everything. I learned my lesson. Can't we try to work this out? We are soul mates and always will be. "I hand over Tyler while I start to cry. "I really loved you." I say. "You hurt us and made us afraid of you. Who does that?" Then I turn away and head to my car as quickly as possible.

A couple more weeks go by and I am still mourning the loss of Nick. Maybe he did finally get the message that he can't treat us like that. I'm tired and I'm really tired of living with my parents. I feel like a little kid with my parents running my life. I know that they mean well, but I do not know how much more that I can take. Maybe Nick and I could work this out. Maybe we could go to counseling. Maybe if I see him one and one and have a true serious conversation he can help me get my own place so we can slowly work on things from a distance. I pick up the phone and decide to make the call. "Okay I am willing if you are. Let's talk about this".

We meet up at a local restaurant/bar and he asked me to bring Tyler with me. I do so. He walks over to my van. My stomach has butterflies all over again. What is it about him that is so addicting. I let him get into the passenger seat of the van. He immediately cups his hands around my face and kisses me. I give in to his kiss. Our tongues feel each other. He then pulls away with tears in his eyes. "I miss you so much." He says. I'm crying at this point too. "I miss you too. Please give me a chance to have my own place so we can work on things slowly." "I will, but you need to make love to me. I need to know that we can do this. Touch me." He says. We are both aroused, but I am feeling insecure and not right about going any farther. Tyler is in the back seat. "Nick please, Tyler is here." "Well, can we at least cuddle in the back seat for a bit? I just want to hold you." I wanted that very much. "But, that is all we are going to do." I say. Tyler is awake and babbling away playing with his toy truck in his car seat. We sit in the back row of the van. His hand is immediately unzipping my pants and then rubbing his fingers over my vulva. I squirm and say. "Nick, no not here please." He can't stop himself. "I know you want this." His fingers are way up inside me now. "Tight and Juicy. That is my T.J." "No" I say. "Tyler is right here." "He's fine." He says while he is sucking away at my neck and ripping my buttons off my shirt. His hand goes right up my bra and he pinches my nipple. "Come on baby. Give it to me. He says. He pushes me down on the seat while he unzips his pants. He yanks my jeans down to my knees. I'm frozen. I just don't know what to do. Tyler starts to fuss, but it doesn't seem to face Nick. He hoists my vagina to his erect penis. He fucks me hard and fast. He is yelling and grunting until he explodes inside of me. Tyler is now screaming from his dad's sexual intoxication. I just want to comfort Tyler, but I wait until he is done and off of me. I feel like a whore. Was I just raped? It's not like I'm going to tell anybody. I'm not even supposed to be here. I really have to get out of here. Nick slaps my thigh. "Amy you will always be the best." Is he even going to give me any money like I asked towards an apartment? "Come home and all of your money worries will be over." He says to me. "I have to get back. My parents will be worried not to mention questionable about where I have been." Nick gets out of the van and lets me get myself dressed and back together." Call me again honey. I will get you some more money. This is all I have on me right now." He says as he hands me two hundred dollars in cash. I feel sick, stupid, not to mention ashamed. I've been gone a long time. What should I say to my parents when I get home? Their one and only rule was that I stay away from Nick.

I pull into the driveway and see that the garage door is open. My parents are standing there waiting for me. My mom is going to know. I can't let anything get past her. She has always caught me in a lie. I never went out at night and left the girls without them knowing where I was going. My hair is matted. I have been crying. It is obvious where I have been. I do not deny it and I say that I am sorry. "You need to get it together Amy. Go say goodbye to your girls." She says to me. "They are leaving to go live with their grandparents in Arizona in the morning. You need to take Tyler and go get a hotel. You can no longer stay here. We hope that you find what you are looking for. We can't live through this again worrying about some stability in their life." I just look at them in shock, but say "okay." A hole is in my heart as I walk downstairs to say goodbye to my girls and how sorry I am for letting them down. I feel like such a failure. My parents are right. I am a mess. They must feel so betrayed after all that they have done for me. I am receiving tough love and I know deep down it's killing them to do it.

As my tears roll down my face I see their tears falling

as well. "Mommy I am going to miss you so much. I don't want to go." Jessica cries out to me. Julienne just turns away from me on the bed. "Girls, mommy is not a strong enough person right now. I need some time to get my life together and you need to be somewhere safe. You guys deserve so much better than this. I will come visit you as soon as I can. I promise." I hold them both and try to stay strong. I kiss them both on the forehead and tell them how much I love them. "I have to go now. Tell Grandma to call me when you get there okay?"

I MOVE IN WITH
MY FRIEND SHEILA

y girls are gone and I settle in with one of my friends. She and her mom said Tyler and I were welcome to live there for a while. I am back in the town of Rochelle once again. I miss my girls terribly. I wish I could just afford a place of my own. But, at the same time I do feel a wave of relief. I know that they are safe and I feel some weight off of my shoulders. We were all uncomfortable living with my parents.

Tyler and I set up our living quarters in the basement. It's not finished, but it is very clean. I went and got our beds out of storage along with a couple night stands. I hang a couple of sheets for a divider between Tyler and I for sleeping arrangements and give us each a little privacy. I have a radio and a couple lamps. I make a trip to Kmart to buy a throw rug for Tyler to play on. I set up a toy box for him to try to make things as homey as possible. I keep our clothes neatly packed in some laundry baskets. It's not home, but at least I have some privacy to think. I need a break from everything.

The first couple nights Tyler would not sleep in his crib. He snuggled next to me with a bottle instead. I feel so depressed. I have to find the energy to find a job. Nick knows how tired I am and that I need his financial help. He is waiting for me to cave. I pick up Tyler and head to my car. I have to get my paperwork in to once again apply for government assistance. I am so tired of doing this, but I don't have a choice. We need to eat, get medical care, and have some cash to get by. Every time that I move I have to start the process all over again or else I will be denied help.

The line is long and Tyler is fussy. I am going to tell them that I still have the girls right now so that I can receive all the help that I can get. When I do get them back I want things to be in order. I am embarrassed when I talk to the social worker. I must look pathetic to her when I explain my insane life and how I got to this point.

"Amy you will have your food stamps and new cards in about a week. You must go to this currency exchange to pick them up along with a check to cash for $200." I feel some relief that there are no problems. "Thank you." I say with tears in my eyes. She smiles and gently grabs my hand. "Can I give you some references for counselors and support groups. It' normal to feel defeated and this could really help to strengthen you. You can't give up. You can only move forward. Your children are counting on you and they will give you the reason to keep going." She has such kindness in her eyes. She must see a lot of this. "Yes please. And thank you for not judging me."

I get Tyler down for a nap and take a walk while my friend Sheila stays with him at the house. I need some air and to just cry my eyes out. I need to get it out. I talk to God and ask him where he is. "I need you now God. Give me the strength that I need. Please direct me on where to go and what to do next." I get to the end of the street next to a cornfield and hear a vehicle slowly creeping up behind me. I turn to look. It's Nick. What a surprise. I knew that this would happen. It was only a matter of time. News travels fast in this little town. He is in a white suit with a hat that makes him look like Al Copone. What is he doing? Has he lost his mind? I feel fear instantly. He is acting weird. He just stares at me. "God you are so beautiful. I miss you so much." He says. "Nick please leave me alone." I say "I will for now. I am here for you honey. Tell me when you are ready to come home." He says with a smirk and a wink. He turns around and drives away just like that. He was driving an SUV that I did not recognize. I'm guessing that his jeep was repossessed. I know that this is not going to stop, but I have nowhere else to go. I just have to deal with it. I still have my order of protection in place. I should have never met up with him. This is could hurt me if he makes an issue out of it. I disobeyed the order myself, but there were no witnesses.

I am back at Sheila's. Her mom is sitting on the couch watching television. "Amy, are you okay hon?" I shake my head with a yes and just head into the kitchen. Sheila is making finger food for her little girl. She turns to look at me and my tears fall once again. I feel so lost inside. I'm tired of being tired. She holds me and says, "We are going out tonight." "Are you sure?" I ask "I don't want to be a burden around here." "Let's go see Peter in the city. From what you have told me about him he really seems to like you. We can go hang out to his favorite bar where we are far away from Nick." I met Peter while I was staying at my parent's house. I was out at an oldies bar on the lake with one of my friends and he hit on me. We have each other's numbers. I guess it couldn't hurt to get out of here for a while. "Okay, let me call him first." I say. "Oh no you don't." She says with a smile on her face. "Surprises are the best. You'll see."

We are on our way to the city and I must admit that I am feeling a little excited and free. We walk into the bar. It's a busy sports bar with all kinds of sports memorabilia on the walls. The owner is great friends with Peter along with many of the Black Hawks. This is the team bar that they hang out at. There is a small dance floor over by the front windows which is not being used right now. The bar is full and many television sets are playing different sports up above.

MOVING ON TO SOMETHING NEW

heila and I find a small table next to the dart boards. She goes to the bar and gets us a couple beers. We sit, drink, and chat. I look around the bar to see if Peter is here. There he is in the back corner. I point him out to Sheila. She smiles back at me. "Not bad. Tall and handsome." "Ya, wait until you hear him talk. He is definitely from the city and an obvious Italian." I reply.

"Go over to him and surprise him. He is not with another girl and he has not spotted us yet." "Okay" I say. "Here goes." I approach him from behind and put my hands gently over his eyes. He turns around quickly. "Oh my God." He says to me with a huge smile. "Surprise." I say with a sweet smile back. I have butterflies in my tummy.

"Thought I would check the place out. Well, actually it was my friend Sheila's idea. I needed a break and I was hoping to run into you."

He follows me over to our table and introduces himself to Sheila. He buys us each another drink and hangs out with us. He seems truly happy to see me. I feel nervous, but at the same time really happy. It's like I'm breathing in fresh air. We play a couple games of darts and I can feel his eyes on me. I can't help but to smile.

When it's time to go home he walks us to our car. Sheila gets in and shuts her door while I stand outside the car to say goodnight to Peter. He leans in without hesitation and kisses me ever so gently. He rubs his hand over my cheek and asks me, "When can I see you again?" "I honestly don't know. I have a one-year-old son and it's hard to get away." He smiles. "Do you like the zoo? We can take him with and grab some dinner. My treat." He says with a smile. I can't turn this offer away. I love the zoo and it would be a perfect place to take Tyler. "Call me tomorrow and we can set it up. I would really like that." I reply with a cute smile and wink. "One more kiss for the road?" he asks. "Of course." This time he gently grabs my face and I let his tongue touch mine. It felt so sensual. I feel liberated once again. I get in the car and we drive away. Sheila says, "See, I told you."

It is one o'clock in the morning when Sheila and I pull into the driveway back at home. I step out of the car and close my door. I hear Nick's voice coming from across the street. "Amy, where have you been? Why aren't you home with our son?" He yells. I turn to look in his direction. I can barely make him out. It's very dark. "Amy, don't talk to him. Come on, let's get inside." Sheila says to me as she grabs my hand and walks me to the door of the house. I knew he was going to do this. This is going to be yet another place that isn't going to work out. He won't leave me alone. I feel afraid, frustrated, angry, and once again defeated.

I head down to the basement. Tyler is sound asleep in his crib. I crawl into my bed as quietly as I can. I look up at the ceiling in deep thought. I need to get a job. How am I going to do that? Who is going to watch Tyler? Can Sheila and I swap schedules? Is it even safe to leave Tyler with anyone else or anywhere else for that matter? I need to get the aide needed from the government for childcare. I feel like I should be the one with him at all times. I'm worried about Nick harassing another caregiver. I'm worried about him taking Tyler when I am not around. This is so unfair.

Sheila is in the kitchen prepping breakfast while her daughter Mandy is crawling on the floor. I let Tyler crawl around with her while Sheila and I talk. "My mom said that Nick was sitting across the street in his SUV on and off the whole time that we were gone last night." Seriously! Are you sure she is still okay with Tyler and I staying here?" I ask with so much frustration on my face. "I can tell that she is nervous about it. She would like you to talk to the police." She tells me while she cuts Mandy's waffle in tiny pieces. "What would Tyler like?" "A waffle is fine." I say with complete sadness in my voice. "He hasn't done anything against the law as of yet. He hasn't physical y hurt me or Tyler. Trust me, Rochelle cops are on his side half of the time. It's like he has them wrapped around his little finger. Maybe he will get bored and give up." Ha, ya right. You are back in town and he is going to watch you like a hawk. He is not going to let you go. He can't handle failure. You are the one who got away." Sheila says to me with her hands on her hips. "You are in danger Amy. He is not in the right mind and he is obsessed with you. You should try to work things out with your parents so you will be better protected. You are welcome to stay here, but I don't think that you will be safe. I can handle his bullshit, but I do not want him to start harassing my mom. I do have the right to call the police on him if I feel that it is necessary and I will have no remorse in doing it." She hugs me and my tears are streaming down my face. "When is his visitation with Tyler again?" She asks me. "We meet at the police station this Friday night at six o'clock. He keeps him until Sunday night at six o'clock." I say. "Peter seems so nice. Have you thought about a relationship with him? He really seems to like you. You have every right to move on Amy. This may be really good for you. I mean, he is already including your son into the game. That says a lot about him. You need to start thinking about your future. Not all men are like Nick Richardson. You could have someone in your life whom will treat you well and will probably protect you." "I have so much baggage Sheila. I'm not sure he would even want to see me anymore after he sees all of this for what it is." "You do have baggage, but you are a beautiful person inside and out. You need to give yourself more credit. You are worthy. He may surprise you. You will never know unless you give it a shot. Maybe this could lead you to get your girls back. I hear you crying at night and I saw the photo album on your bed. Sorry, I do not mean to pry, but I know that you are missing them terribly." "Okay, fine. I will set up a date. We can go back to the city Saturday night while Nick has

Tyler." I say as I give in. I am desperate for any kind of relief at this point.

I do not know what emotion that I'm feeling from one hour to the next as the day goes on. I just want to be happy. I am worried about money and where I am going to end up next. I wish that I did not have to rely on anyone. I just want my life back. I want my home, my own bed, my girls, a routine, and most importantly some kind of peace. Why do I have to go through all of this? Nick still gets to live in our house.

LIFE BEGINS A NEW CHAPTER

eter and I have been on many dates now. His mom watches Tyler for me a lot which is good because she lives in the city and it is not convenient for Nick to bother me. Nick has been pretty quiet for about a month now. He does not know where I have been staying. I'm having fun, making new friends, and even got to dance with the referee from the Black Hawks. I'm still missing my girls terribly. Each time that I talk to them on the phone, my heart aches. The tears fall for a good hour after talking to them. Peter has been very understanding and supportive of this whole situation.

"Amy, I want to send you and Tyler to see your girls. Because I work for American Airlines I can get you tickets very cheap. You would have to fly standby. It's my treat. You need to see them." Peter says to me while we are eating dinner at Wendy's. Tyler is in a high chair throwing all of his food on the floor. It doesn't even seem to faze Peter. He is a father as well to a son who lives with his mother the majority of the time in Wisconsin. Peter meets her half way every other weekend to pick him up. "Oh my God! That would mean the world to me." I say with excitement. "When you get back from Arizona I want to talk to you about some things. I want to help you. I love you Amy." He says to me. How can this man love me? My life is such a mess. It is so much for him to take on. I am not in love with him, but I'm sure that could change in time. I have just been so protective of my feelings. When we make love it does not feel like that in love feeling. It feels like safety, compassion, and warmth. I know he is feeling more for me than I do for him. As weird as it is, I do still think about Nick in that way. He and I did have an amazing sex life at times that took me to amazing places. This just doesn't compare and I do not know how to feel about it. Why can't I get over this asshole? I'm afraid of him, but at the same time I'm addicted to him. What in God's name is wrong with me? And, what if I can't give Peter back what he gives me?

I land in Arizona. I can feel the heat as I exit the plane into the terminal. Tyler slept most of the flight so he is in good spirits. We are to meet the girls and their grandparents in baggage claim. My heart is going a million miles an hour. It's been a few months since I have seen them. I can't wait to see them. I miss them so much. As we come down the escalator I spot them to the right. They are dressed up in beautiful dresses. Their hair is curled. I have such beautiful girls. Their grandma has always loved to get them all dolled up and spoil them rotten. They see Tyler and I. They come running at full speed. "Mommy!" they fall in into my arms. "We missed you so much!" Their hugs are the size of Mount Everest. This is the best feeling ever. I want them back.

We stay at their grandparent's house for the week. Even though their son and I have divorced, they still treat me like family. They even let me use one of their cars to take the kids out. I'm glad that Peter gave me some spending money to take them out to do some fun stuff. During the day we use the pool out back, do some shopping, make crafts, and cuddle to movies and popcorn at night. Julienne and I always did crafts together back home. It's one of her favorite things to do. The girls draw me pictures and make me cards to take back home with me. I get many pictures of them. I want to see their faces every day. I take in every moment that I can.

The week has flown by. It is time for me to say goodbye once again. We are back at the airport and the girls and I are in tears. I hug them one last time. This is not right. It's time for me to get my shit together no matter what it takes. They belong with me. Tyler and I board the plane and get settled in our seats. I can't stop crying. The stewardess asked if I'm going to be okay. I nodded my head to let her know I'll be okay. "Just had to say goodbye to my girls." I tell her. I then tend to Tyler giving him a snack. I'm emotionally drained.

BACK HOME

eter is waiting for Tyler and I in baggage claim. He knows that I am devastated leaving my girls behind. He hugs me and says "Welcome back." "Thank you for sending me to see them." I say with a small smile and tears just running down my face. He grabs Tyler from me and says, "Let's go back to my mom's so you can rest. I'll keep Tyler busy and later we can talk about some things. "Okay that sounds nice." I say quietly.

Tyler is giggling in the kitchen while Peter and his mom entertain him. I walk in to see my little stinker having so much fun that he doesn't even notice me. Peter looks up at me and asks, "Did you have a nice nap?" "Yes I very much needed that. Thank you." I look at how he and his mom are really enjoying having a little guy around. It warms my heart and helps me to relax. "My mom is watching Tyler tonight. I would like to take you out for a nice Italian dinner." "Okay that sounds nice."

Peter knows the owner of this restaurant and we are treated like royalty. This is upper class. Candles are glowing on top of white table cloths. It must be an Italian thing. Peter grabs my hand. He looks at me with kindness and love in his heart. "I want to make this a better situation for you and for us." He starts out. "I want Nick to leave you alone and I want you to live somewhere safe; not in Rochelle. My friend Tom has an extra room. He and I would both like you to stay there with Tyler. I do not want you to tell anyone where you are staying except your parents. I would also like us to get a place together so we can get your girls back home. I need to get some money together first. I also need to make sure my Ma and sister are taken care of first. With my ma taking care of a disabled daughter, she will still need some extra help." His sister is wheel chair bound with cerebral palsy. She requires twenty four hour care. "I am in love with you and I want to be with you. I really want to get to know your girls and give them a home with us." I'm overwhelmed. I want that too. But I know my feelings for him are not as strong as his are for me. I feel guilty, but I consider this as a good thing and I feel hope. I can make it work. I will have all of my children back home safely with me. I agree to the plan. I hold his hand tightly and say, "Thank you." I'm very lucky to have someone so loving and caring.

Tom's place is here in the north part of the city right off of the expressway. Oh'Charlies restaurant is walking distance along with the L. Tom uses the L for transportation to and from work. He works at Ohare airport for American Airlines just like Peter. Tom and I have met a couple of times when we were out at the bar. He is very kind. He does love his booze though. He does love to go out with the guys and does not spend very much time at home which could be a good thing for Tyler and I. Tom is at work now, but Peter has a key to get us settled in. "He is definitely a bachelor isn't he?" I say with a chuckle. We are in a third story tan brick apartment. There are rows and rows of these apartments. There is a nice park in the middle of the buildings. I am looking at the window of the building across from me. I could literally hold a conversation with my neighbor. I feel no privacy here. I really hate the city. But, at least I will be safe and I do not have to worry about how to pay for it. There is no furniture except for the television in the living room and Tom's bedroom. I will need all of my furniture from Sheila's. "Looks like I'll be making a few trips to Rochelle to get my stuff." "Yes we are going to get your things this afternoon. You are not going alone. This is your new home for a while. It's not paradise, but it is safe and temporary. I'll be close by and Tome will be around as well to protect you." "I hope Nick does not find this place." I say. "I'm sure that he will eventually, but this buys us some time to find a permanent home for us. If he does show up here he will have hell to pay. I will not put up with his bullshit. This is my side of town now. He would be messing with the wrong people. I have many friends." He says with a smile. "Well this is it. Thank you for all of this. Let's go get my things." I give him a kiss.

I'm settled in. Tyler is cruising around the apartment pushing one of his trucks. I try to make the place as homey as I can. I decorate the bedroom. I put up some pictures and get our beds put together. I even put outlet covers on the outlets around the apartment. At least Tom has cable in the living room so I put some cartoons on for Tyler. Tom is at work. It is nice to have some time to myself. He is not the cleanest person. I scrub the bathroom and kitchen. He does not cook, so at least I know that I can be of some help making homemade meals for the three of us. I once again have to go to public aid downtown in the city to get all my government aid once again. God, how many times am I going to have to do this?

I find a new job at Target while Peter's mom cares for Tyler. I have to drop him off at 6:30 every morning. I hate the job. I have to clean the store every morning. I learn to operate the floor buffer. Cleaning all of the toilets is gross. My schedule is regular and works out for Tyler's sake. I don't have a lot of skills or a college education. I have to do what I have to do. For now this will work. I have to start making some money. The only time that I see any child support money is when I have to go back to court. I always go into the court main office to pick it up because Nick is forced to pay right then and there or face being arrested. It sucks that I have to keep going back to Rochelle to court to get him to pay. I know that it's just a game that he plays and he knows that he can get away with it. He also knows how hard it is for me to hold down a job when I have to take off all of the time to go there. It's all about his control over me.

Peter always goes with me to exchange Tyler. I stay in the car while Peter goes into the police station to hand him over. I know this has to be killing Nick. He can't have contact with me and he is seeing me with another man. When we leave we take different routes home to throw him off in case he tries to follow us.

WE ARE FOUND

t's early evening and I'm putting laundry away in our dresser. Tyler and I share a dresser since we don't have much room. I hear something hit the bedroom window. I'm three floors up. Maybe it's a bird. I hear it again. What the heck? I walk over to the window and look out. Nick is throwing stones at the window. He sees me look out and then starts yelling at the top of his lungs. "Amy I have a right to know where my son lives. It's not okay for you to hide him from me. I'm still his father and I will always find you!" I can't believe this. It's only been two months and he found me. That's it! I need to call the police. He must be under the influence to make such a scene. I'm embarrassed, angry, and scared.

I call the police. By the time they show up he is nowhere to be found. I show them all of the order of protections I have had on him. They put everything on record and then tell me to take the information to the courthouse downtown and write a formal statement for the court records. The more information that you have the better you have for your case. I'm told to reinstate my order of protection with the Chicago court system.

After they leave I call Peter to tell him what has just happened. "This guy doesn't know who he is fucking with. I am going to take care of this." He says with stern anger in his voice. "How are you going to do that?" I ask. "I know people that can teach him a lesson and they have already been put on call for me." "What will they do?" "He may not be able to walk soon. Put it that way." Oh God I think to myself. This is illegal and it scares me. "No Peter. I don't want any of us to end up in jail. Please there has to be another way."

Peter did not send anybody to pay him a visit, but he did call him to have a little chat. He warned him and made sure he understood that I was no longer his property. I do not know what he threatened to do to him and honestly I don't want to know.

It's been quiet for a week now. Nick has not been around that I know of. I get nervous every time that I walk to my car and while I'm driving. I'm always on guard. This morning I take Tyler with me to the car to get his stroller out of the trunk. It's sunny and warm enough to get out and take him to the park. As I am walking up to my car I notice a dildo hanging on my antenna. "What the fuck?' I say out loud. There is not a note, but I know it was Nick. Only he would do something like this the way that his mind thinks. I can't prove this, but I am going to make sure that I write everything down with dates to keep track of things that happen. I am pissed off, but I am still going to take my son to the park. If I see him I will scream at the top of my lungs. This is a populated area. Somebody would call 911 for sure. I can't live my life like this.

I take Tyler to the park. He loves the baby swing. He giggles every time I tap his toes with each swing. He keeps saying "More!" every time the swing starts to slow down. I let him run around to burn off some of his energy and then I put him back in his stroller for a nice long walk. When we get back to the apartment I decide that I am going to check my mail. There are four cards to me from Nick. I recognize his hand writing on the envelopes. I take them upstairs and open them. They all say that I love you, miss you, and you will always be mine. I can't live without you, etc. ending with his famous signature (Love your favorite ex-husband). I'm not going to tell Peter about these right now. I hide them safely in the back of my closet instead. I am going to go about my business and ignore everything that Nick is trying to do to me. I will have the cards with postmark dates for future reference.

It's a new day. I have finished another's day work. I'm moving on period. It's a normal day just like any other. Peter works evenings, but he usually stops by after work to spend some time with me on his way home. I have to go to bed early so he doesn't hang around for very long, but I still enjoy the company. I feel lonely a lot of the time living here. I don't see any friends or family right now. On my way up to my apartment I stop to the check the mail. I just happen to run into the mailman. He has six priority envelopes to give me. It's Nick's writing again. The mailman asks, "Is everything alright. This appears pretty obsessive. Are you in any danger?" he asks me. "Uhg, this guy is nuts. No, I'm alright. He is just messing with me. I'll call the police if this continues." I reply. I take the envelopes upstairs and I open them. One envelope has a sexy set of underwear. Another envelope has $500.00 in cash. Another envelope has photos of our wedding. The other two envelopes have a necklace and earrings in one and in the other has a gift card to a local spa. I hide all of these in the closet too.

The next evening I receive a pizza from Dominoes. Nick wrote on the inside cover of the box (I know you miss me). This continues for the rest of the week with more messages inside the boxes. I lay them down on the kitchen floor and snap pictures of everything. I need to get these developed to put in my case file. I then call the police to come take a look at everything so documentation can be made.

It's the next morning. I get my pictures developed and head to the courthouse. I'm angry that I have to go through all of this especially carrying a toddler around. After waiting two hours for my turn to be called and trying to keep my son from throwing fits I walk up to the counter and request a new restraining order that includes him not seeing Tyler. I am trying to eliminate any contact at this point. The order of protection is granted no problem.

I call Peter when I get home to fill him in on everything. He is not happy that I have been keeping all of this from him. He wants to talk tonight about a new game plan. I wonder what he means by this. This is so hard for me. Nick has sent me all of this stuff. He has not hurt me. I'm scared in one sense, but he is once again making me miss him. I miss being spoiled by him. He is sick and has a problem. He just needs to get some help. I know I can't feel these feelings, but I know that I will never love Peter the way that I loved him. Nick is being so persistent. He can't let me go and he is making it very hard for me to let him go. I really loved him and I still miss the good times. When things were good between us, it was the happiest time of my life. The highs I felt with Nick are unexplainable. Others around me would think I'm crazy if they knew I was having these feelings. It's an addiction that nobody can understand. I feel guilty for having these feelings. I'm actually worried about him. What the hell is wrong with me? Why can't I just let go and move on. It's because he won't let me.

NEW GAME PLAN

eter and I talk over drinks. Tyler is sound asleep. He wants me to look for a new place for us to move in together. "I want to be able to protect you and let you have your family back together. I want you to be in my arms in bed every night. Let's get things rolling so we can get your girls back home. "Peter I don't want my kids living in the city. I don't like it here. This is not a good place to raise my kids." He then gets me to see his perspective and the positive points of staying out this way, but I still refuse. "I want to live by my mom." I say. He gives in. It will be an hour drive for him to go to work, but he is willing. At least his schedule does not coincide with rush hour traffic. I'm nervous about the whole situation, but I want my girls back. They need to be with me even if I'm not 100% happy. Things don't have to be perfect. Everyone has to make sacrifices at some point. Who knows, maybe over time my feelings for him will grow stronger. He is a good man who is good looking and has my best interests at heart. I don't have any other options at this point. It would be nice to take my time, but the situation is not allowing it. I should be blessed and grateful. "My mom and I will start looking for a place in her area. The nice thing is that it is cheaper to live out that way and my parents can help out with the kids. When we find something that I like I will set it up for us to look at."

We move into a cute ranch in a town next to my parent's. The girls have their own room, Tyler has his, we have ours, and there is even an office downstairs. It's clean and updated. The rent is reasonable. Peter's friend keeps a boat here on the Chain O Lakes which is a plus. My girls are coming home in two weeks.

"Before your girls come home I have one more special surprise for you." Peter says to me. I look at him in anticipation. As Peter and I have gotten to know each other the subject of my natural father has come up many times. He knows that my father gave me up for adoption to my step dad when I was nine years old. It's a very hard topic for me to talk about. I have never gotten over it. I wouldn't be surprised this is the reason that I have ended up in unhealthy relationships. A father plays a big role in a daughter's life to lead her in the right direction especially when it comes to men. I do need answers as to why he gave me up so easily. "I am sending you and Tyler to visit your father to have your questions answered. You need some closure and I know how much pain he has caused you. Find him in LaCrosse and see if he will welcome you." Wow, I think to myself. He has the means to send me and he is right. I accept his offer. "It's also a good thing for you to disappear for a bit so Nick will be thrown off on your whereabouts."

I find my father through my aunt. She relays the message to him. He contacts me personally by phone and he wants to see me. I can't believe it. Even his wife who has never wanted me around agreed. I know my father gave me up because of her. She couldn't handle my presence when I was a little girl. I was my mother's daughter and part of his past. The visitations stopped and he gave up his rights to me shortly after. One afternoon I watched out our sliding glass doors waiting for him to come pick me up. It was then the phone call was received and my mom had to break the news to me that my father was never coming back.

We set up the date of my flight out there. Tyler and I stay at my father's home for three days. I'm glad I went to see him, but I do not leave satisfied. I did get to meet my half siblings and get a lot off my chest. His answers to me still did not justify his choices. I was his daughter period. I'm second place to his new family and always will be. But, like Peter said; I did get some closure out of the visit. I am grateful for this gift that he has given me. I can move on from it now. Someday I will write my story of why a father's love is so important to a daughter's development.

THE GIRLS ARE COMING HOME!

We go together to pick up my girls from the airport. I'm so excited. I have not been able to sit still or eat a thing all day. This is such a happy day in my life. On the way home the girls talk our ears off about school and their friends in Arizona. They do not appear disturbed by Peter's presence. They have never met him, but they don't seem to care. I can tell they are happy to be back home with me. "I can't wait to see our new house." Jessica says wiggling in her seat with anticipation. "Me too!" Julienne says. "I think they are going to be two very happy girls." I say as Peter and I smile at each other while he holds my hand in the car.

I have the girls enrolled in their new schools. They make

friends very quickly. We are all getting along well and they appear very happy and content. Life is good. I'm still not in love with Peter, but I am content with things. He wants to take me out to dinner tonight." I have something that I would like to talk to you about. Dress up nice. This is a special occasion." He says to me.

We are out to dinner at another nice Italian restaurant of course. We are settled in a nice booth enjoying a couple cocktails. "Well, what do you want to talk about." I ask. He reaches in his pocket and pulls out a beautiful ring. "Amy, marry me." I knew this was coming sooner or later. I do not feel ready for this step, but I want my life to be stable. "We are a family now. My son loves you and the girls. It's time to make this permanent. I can give us a good life and love you the way that you should be loved." I agree to marry him. This is my new life now. It's a good life.

We marry in Vegas two months later. Just the two of us go. I'm feeling overwhelmed. This is happening way too fast. It's like I don't have time to absorb what is happening. I'm just doing it and going with the flow. I have all of my children back in one house. That is all that matters right now.

The day we marry we make love in our hotel room. Peter then falls asleep. I can't sleep. I sit up looking out the window at all of the lights in the city that never sleeps. I feel a sense of sadness. This is it. I am now officially committed and trapped. We are husband and wife. It doesn't feel right in my gut. I'm suddenly paralyzed with a feeling of panic. What did I just do? I sit there and cry while I look over at Peter sleeping. I had no choice. This is what I had to do. It's my third marriage for Christ's sake. We can't have everything we want right? I can't help but to think about my wedding night with Nick. I felt so fulfilled and happy on that day. I was so in love with him and deep down I still miss him.

Life begins as an official family. I am back to cleaning houses to help with the bills. I am working for myself and making some good cash money. Peter and I swap shifts with the kids. It's working out I guess. He sleeps later so I take care of Tyler for an hour every morning. I then put him back in his crib when I have to leave. I hate doing this. I feel horrible guilt when I put him back in there. I know he is going to be sitting there for a while until Peter gets up with him. I walk in the bedroom to say goodbye to Peter and let him know the girls are ready for school. He is snoring and drooling all over his pillow. I feel grossed out by this. My feelings for him are dwindling. I feel guilty for feeling this way, but I really don't know how long I can do this.

Peter and I have plans for a night out. My parents have the kids for the night. We are going to go into the city to see friends. I come down the stairs dressed and ready to go. "Oh no, you are my wife now. You are not going out wearing that." I'm in a blouse and spandex pants. I'm thinking What the hell? You don't own me. "Why?" I ask. "Everyone will be checking your ass out. It's not appropriate." I'm not happy, but I do not want to get into an argument so I go put some jeans on instead.

We make it into the city and go to our famous hangout on Harlem Avenue. Peter stays right by me and watches me like a hawk. He gets aggravated when another unknown gentleman starts to talk to me at the bar. "Hey, this is my wife. Back off and mind your own business." He says to him. It is at this moment that I know that I am screwed. I left one controlling man for another one. At least I loved Nick. I made my bed. Now I'm lying in it.

TIME FOR THERAPY

ver since I got my order of protection in Chicago I have not been bothered by Nick. He has not seen Tyler in quite a while. It does seem too quiet for him. As sick as this sounds I miss his persistence to get me back. Deep down I am still missing him. I keep reminiscing about the good times. It's amazing how you can let the bad things go over time. He wasn't always crazy. Maybe he got clean and straightened his act out. I could never share this with Peter. It would crush him. I think I need to talk to a professional. I need help at this point. I am going to drive myself crazy.

I found a therapy group to join for abused women. I need to go. I need to know that I am not crazy. I don't know what to do with my feelings anymore. Is there still any happiness out there for me? I do not tell Peter about this. I need to deal with this on my own right now.

"Everyone we have a new member to our group. This is Amy. Let's welcome her to our group." says the therapist. Everyone in the group says hello and welcome. We all gather together in a circle facing each other. Everyone introduces themselves to me and I reply with a quiet hello. I feel so nervous. My intestines are rumbling. Having irritable bowel syndrome in circumstances such as this can be so embarrassing. I tell myself to just calm down and relax. I take in a few deep breaths and let them back out slowly.

"Amy you do not have to say anything if that is what you choose. Feel free to just listen and get to know the group. We want you to feel comfortable. This is a safe place and we support each other." says the therapist. "Okay." I reply. I hear everyone's story. A couple girls were hospitalized by their abusers. I think to myself that my situation was not that bad. I am rationalizing Nick's past behavior. Then a couple of the other women talk about the mind games of mental abuse that they suffered. The therapist reassures us that this is not love or normal behavior. This kind of behavior is used to control us. It affects our confidence and makes us question ourselves. We think that we are not good enough and we can't make decisions for ourselves. We are taught to believe that we can't make it on our own and we need our abuser to survive. This is how they control us." She explained the cycle of abuse. "They scare us to submit to their ways. We lose ourselves in order to live for them. We often forget who we are and eventually think this is normal." I suddenly speak up. "But why do we still love them? And why can't we let them go?" Another woman speaks up. "Honey we all loved our abusers. We didn't meet them as an abuser. We fell in love with them for a reason. They knew exactly what to say and do when we needed it. Their charm made us head over heels. We want to experience that again and we want to believe that it's temporary and they will come to their senses. But honey, I got news for you. They don't." another woman steps in to say. "I dropped my orders of protection three times because I believed that he had changed only to find out each time I did it the abuse got worse." "Why do I feel my situation is still different? Nick is just mentally ill. There is a reason for his behavior. It's not always his fault." "Honey, you are kidding yourself. We all want to believe that there is a reason that they are acting this way and it can be fixed. They are who they are. They are not safe. They do not know what love is and they do not change." My tears are welling up. I try to hold them back, but I can't. The woman next to me gives me a box of Kleenex and tells me to let it out. "Honey this is why we are here. We all have felt these feelings at some point. Some of us still do just like you. It's even harder if they are the father to our children. We are all in the same boat. You have to make that conscious choice to let go and move on. It is then that you will become strong and whole once again."

I fall into her arms and let my tears soak her shirt. "Thank you." I say. She pulls a pen and notepad out of her purse and starts writing. "Here is my phone number. You can call me anytime."

On my way home I pulled the car over and just broke down. I let every tear out that I could. I yelled and screamed while beating on my steering wheel. I will go back to group. I have to. I feel like this is never going to get any easier.

It's a beautiful weekend. We have plans for our friends to come over to celebrate our new life as husband and wife. It's really more of his friends and family than mine. We party, get silly, and open all of our gifts in the garage. Fall season has hit and we wanted to be prepared for the seasonal weather changes. Today is a perfect sixty five degrees and sunny. We are all having a nice time, but I'm not feeling the happiness that Peter is. He is over the moon and feels so complete inside. I feel like I'm just sitting in playing a role. "Anybody need anything?" I ask before I go hide inside the house for a while. I do not feel like entertaining at this point. I just want to be alone in my thoughts. Nobody even hears me or is paying attention to my request so I head into the house.

I walk down our hallway. Julienne is on the floor in her bedroom drawing as usual. She is my little artist and so talented. Tyler is still napping in his crib. I walk into our bedroom and sit on the bed. I stare at the closed closet doors for I don't even know how long. I'm in a trance. I want to fly away to a happy place. "Mom, are you coming back outside? Peter is looking for you?" I turn to look over at my sweet Jessica standing in the doorway. "Ya baby, I'm coming. Just give me a few minutes. I'm just really tired and I am taking a little time out."

Everyone has finally left and Peter helps me clean up. I did a lot of prepping for the party and he thanks me. "My friends really like you and they are very happy for us." He says to me while he turns me towards him and looks me in the eyes. "I love you Amy." He is so good to me and my kids. "I love you too." I say back because I know that's what he wants to hear. He kisses me and hints to have some fun in the bedroom tonight after the kids are down. His son is with us for the weekend as well so it will be a while before that can happen. "We will see." I say with a cute smile. When we started dating I loved the sex. I was in with drawl and the sex made me feel better mentally and physically, but now I'm already bored with it. There is no intensity in it for me. I have no desire anymore. I struggle with these feelings. I feel so much guilt for feeling this way. I can't force my mind to accept everything for what it is. I have to pretend. He is a handsome, caring, protective, loving to my children, and he provides for our needs. Why can't I just be happy with this and move on? It's a constant battle in mind. I jumped into this relationship faster than I had wanted to. I have to suck it up. My choices are made. I'll have a few more cocktails to get myself in the mood.

I freshen myself up. Stephen is asleep on the floor with the girls with a movie playing in the background downstairs. Popcorn and Nintendo game controllers are scattered around them. I'm glad that they all get along. Stephen and Julienne are close in age which does help. They all seem quite comfortable. I don't see any point in waking them. I turn off the lights and head back upstairs. I check on Tyler. He is sound asleep with a blanket covering his head. I'm sure Peter is waiting patiently for me to come to bed. I walk into our bedroom and feel relieved. He is snoring heavily. It must be from all of those beers earlier. I decide to go back into the living room and grab myself another cocktail. I can't sleep right now. I pull out my photo albums. The tears and running down my face. "Damn you Nick. Why did you have to ruin everything?" I cry out. I want the intense high of having such strong feelings for someone again. My heart aches for it. I want that kind of passion back in my life. I want to feel that high again. I'm starving for it despite the danger involved. What the fuck is wrong with me?

It's the weekend of Halloween. The kids and I buy our pumpkins at the local grocery store. "I want the gigantic one over there mom." Julienne says jumping up and down with excitement. "Okay, pick one out for Tyler and Stephen too please. Jessica, which one do you want?" She picks a smaller round cute one right in front of her. "Mom, you have to get one too." She says. I smile. "Well of course I do." This is bringing back the memories of Nick and I taking all three girls to the pumpkin patch, eating donuts, drinking cider, and finally hitting the corn maze. We did make some wonderful memories with the kids. We were always on the go with something new to do almost every day. I miss those times and I want them back.

When we get home I check the mail. There is an envelope from an attorney's office in Rochelle. Oh boy, I think. This is probably not good. Nick and his attorney had been up in front of a judge to get his visitation rights back. There is a new order to meet Nick at the Rochelle police station to exchange Tyler for visits every other weekend. I can fight this, but I have to contact an attorney so a new court date can be set. Until then I have to follow the order or face arrest. I do not have the time or money to fight this. I am back to work now and I'm tired of the financial loss to deal with this. Peter is going to love hearing this. He is going to be so angry. Then again, maybe things can go smoothly. Nick has appeared to settle down. He has not violated the order of protection or bothered me. He does love his son and I do not believe he would ever hurt him. I could use the break on those weekends. Taking care of toddler is a lot of work and Tyler isn't the easiest child to deal with. His temper tantrums are getting bad. It can be quite exhausting.

It's Nick's weekend to have Tyler. Peter usually goes with me. This weekend he has to go see his mom about his sister's care plan. Nick notices that he is not with me for the exchange this time. He looks at me in the parking lot. He has tears in his eyes. He walks up to my car slowly. "Amy, I don't want to hurt you. Can we please just talk?" I want to talk to him. I want him to hold me and tell me this is all a bad dream. Being in his presence right now I feel no fear but rather love. I know that I should not do this, but I get out and stand next to my car. I am in a police station parking lot. I mean what can he do here? Tyler is asleep in his car seat. Nick gently touches my face and cups the back of my head. He moves in the kiss me. I don't pull away. I want him. His kiss makes me weak at the knees. My tummy flips. It feels so good. He kisses slow with passion. I let my tongue slither with his. He pulls himself away and looks at me with those beautiful blue eyes. "I love you Amy. There will never be another you. Nobody can replace you. You are my soul mate. I know that you don't feel this way with Peter. You can feel it too. I can tell by the way you kissed me back. I will never hurt you again. I've had so much time to think about everything that I have put you through. I promise! I have learned so much about anger management. I have proof of all the counseling that I have been through. I had to prove it to the judge to see my son again. I was wrong. I'm so sorry. Please come back to me."

It's happening again. I really believe him this time. We have been apart for almost a year now. He has been working hard to get better. He has been following all of the rules in our court paperwork and actually paying his child support on time. Tyler loves seeing him. "How am I supposed to do that? I am married to someone else now. The kids are thriving." He is right. I am not happy. I did make a huge mistake marrying Peter. I know that in my heart. Can Nick and I try one more time? Will the kids be okay with this? I know how much better of a mom that I can be if I am happy. I'm scared. My parents will disown me. In my heart I want this more than anything. In time maybe my family can get over it once they see the change in him. We could have are whole family back together again. The girls and I miss having Marley around. Maybe it really is the right time for him to make things right for all of us. "Marry me again. I will make things right this time. You can divorce Peter in no time. We can start over in a new home. My business is coming back together. I'm clean now. Amy, you make me a better man. I didn't do this for me, but I got better for our whole family."

My head is spinning. I want this, but I really have to think about it. "I lost my girls because of you and I just got them back. I don't want to lose them again. And, I would have to sit down with them and talk about it. Their feelings matter too. I do still love you and miss you." He looks at me kindly and says, "I know my girl. When she wants something she will go get it. This is what I love about you. I have faith in the man upstairs Would you like to get some dinner; just the three of us right now. I will take you to Olive Garden. It's your favorite."" No, my parents are waiting on me to pick up the girls and Peter is waiting for me to get back. He will be very suspicious and concerned." "Okay, see if you can get away on Sunday when you take Tyler back. I know that you want to."

I get Tyler out of the car and hand him over. He is so happy to see his dad. They go on their way. On my way home my heart is beating so fast. I can't believe that I am considering doing this. I feel elated and full of life once again. I do not want to stay with Peter.

I pull into our driveway. I need to compose myself before I go into the house. Deep breaths, here I go. As I walk in I hear the cartoons playing on the TV upstairs. Peter picked up the girls since he got back into town early. I can also hear Peter talking to somebody on the phone in the basement. It sounds like he is making bets for the next football game. I know that he gambles and it's not in small amounts. It's, another thing that I am not very hip on. We are not exactly rich. We have stopped at many phone booths while he takes the newspaper with him. He actually asked me to consider being a bookie for easy money. It's more like illegal money.

The girls are giggling and teasing each other. I know that they are enjoying a break from their little brother. "Mom!" they yell as they run up to me. "Can we make cookies tonight? Please, please, please." They squeal. "Sure, we can do that. I'll be ready in a few minutes. Mommy needs to get into something comfortable and make a glass of wine." Julienne goes to the kitchen cabinets and starts to pull out all of the ingredients. Jessica gets out the bowls, spoons, and cookie sheets. I could actually use this distraction right now.

As we are in the process of our cookie making, Peter makes his way upstairs and into the kitchen. "How did it go today exchanging Tyler? Were there any problems?" "Really good actually. He was very nice. There were no problems at all." Please don't ask me anymore I think to myself. It's hard to keep a straight face. I hate to lie. "That's good to hear." He replies. "Will you be okay from now on if I am not with you when you meet him?" I think he is tired of having to go which is fine with me. "Sure, I should be fine. We are at a police station so I feel safe." That's a relief to me. The girls and I continue our cookie making while Peter goes back downstairs to make some phone calls and pay some bills.

It's late. Peter and I are lying in bed. I don't feel like talking so I reach for my book. "Tyler is not here so we don't have to get up early tomorrow. Want to have some fun?" He asks while he is fondling my breasts. I don't want to have sex. All I can think about is Nick. I can't wait to see him again. This is such a mess. I kiss his forehead and say, "I have a lot on my mind and I'm really tired. Tomorrow, maybe?" He rolls away from me and turns out his light. I know that I hurt his feelings. Five minutes later his snoring begins. Now I am annoyed. I get out of bed and go downstairs. I can't believe that I am about to do this. I dial his number. I'm a nervous wreck, but I feel like a teenager with anticipation and excitement. I know as the phone is ringing that he knows it's me calling. The area code alone is a dead giveaway. "Hey honey! I knew I would hear from you. We are destined to be together." He says with his usual chuckle. "How are you? You miss me don't you?" "I love you Nick. I wish that I didn't, but I do and I miss you very much. I miss our good times. I don't know what to do anymore. This is such a mess. You are right. I do not love Peter. I'm depressed. If I leave him my family will disown me. If I'm with you my parents will never forgive me for everything that I have put them through. I'm scared to do anything. And how do I know if you will never hurt the kids or I again?"

"Amy, I no longer use any drugs, I went to classes, and I am rebuilding my business. I'm even going to church. Give me a chance to make things up to you guys. I can't change what I did in the past, but I can make things right. I love you so much. I want to give you the life that you deserve. I was so wrong. I learned horrible things from my father, and in turn followed in his footsteps. This is why my anger came out on him the way that it did. Taking care of him was a stressor on both of us which didn't help things. I understand now how badly that I scared and hurt you. I don't own you. You are your own person and I am to respect that. You are smart and talented. I did not appreciate or honor you. I learned this in my anger management classes. I am so sorry Amy. Please forgive me. We can continue to go to church together as a family. We can rebuild everything. Don't worry about money to move. Your family will come around once they see us happy. You just have to give them time. It will all be okay."

I am so tempted to just pick up and go. I just want to be happy. I believe him this time. He has changed. God forgives. Why can't I? I still love him. I can't make that disappear no matter how hard I try. Lord help me with this. What should I do? "The girls are going to Arizona next weekend to visit their father. They have Friday and Monday off of school so it will be a long weekend away from them. We can get together one of those nights when Peter is at work. We can do something fun with Tyler." I say to him. I figure this way Peter won't know about the visit and being in a public place with Tyler would be a great place to start. Let's talk about it when we exchange Tyler on Sunday. How does that sound?" I ask him. "I can't wait. I love you Amy." "Give Tyler lots of hugs and kisses from me. See you Sunday." I say. We hang up. Oh my God. I'm doing this. I feel really good about this. I really do. I have actual butterflies in my stomach. I won't be able to sleep tonight. True love just can't be torn apart.

If this goes in the direction that I want it to, I will have to eventually tell the girls. They will be very confused. They may even be scared or angry. I can't be a good mother to them unless I'm happy and healthy. And right now at this moment I am so happy. I have to keep cool and act normal around Peter. I don't even know how I would break this news to him. He has done so much for me and my children, but this was rushed and I felt so pressured to marry him in the first place. I'm grateful for everything that he has done for me and the kids, but I do not love him. I just don't!

I'm waiting to board the girls on the plane to see their father. The flight has been delayed. Tyler is climbing all over me and crawling under the chairs. As I am keeping all of my children occupied, I'm imagining my date with Nick tonight. I am so excited. Tyler and I will be meeting him at our favorite Japanese restaurant. Tyler will love watching the sliced onion volcano go up in flames. The fiery volcano never gets dull for children. Finally….."Now boarding rows twenty three through twenty six." It's time to walk the girls up to the line. "I'll miss you guys. I will see you in a few days. I love you." We give our hugs and kisses and off they go. "Come on Tyler. Let's go see your daddy." I say to him with a smile.

WE TRY AGAIN

'm dressed in a cute outfit with my hair in a loose French braid. Nick has always loved my hair like this. I don't want to overdress and look too obvious to Peter. I put on my jeans with a cute tan turtle neck sweater. I throw on some adorable penny loafers and some cheap jewelry. I have Tyler in his cute Bulls outfit that his father gave him a while back.

I pull into the parking lot and there he is waiting in his work van. I pull up next to him. Tyler starts kicking with excitement when he sees his daddy. This is how I want things to be. I want my family back together. Nick opens Tyler's door. "Hey buddy, are you happy to see me" Tyler smiles and shakes his head to say yes. Nick unbuckles him from his car seat and picks him up. Tyler hugs him tight with his silly little giggle. "Want some steak and shrimp buddy? You and your mommy only deserve the best." Nick hugs me from the side and kisses my cheek" I'm so happy you came." He says to me. "Hey Japanese food; I'm in." I say with my cute little smile.

Nick orders us two pina coladas with 151 rum in them and a kiddy cocktail for Tyler. "Surf and turf honey?" He asks me. "Well dah." I say laughing. It's nice being with somebody who knows me inside and out. Tyler is sitting in his booster seat between us. I always bring a sippy cup of juice along with some cherrios or crackers to occupy him. Tonight I brought him gold fish which is his favorite. As he munches away Nick holds my hand. He looks me in the eyes. "I miss you. Come home." He says with such sincerity. I want to go home. I want this madness to be over. We belong together. We understand each other. That is it. I am going to tell the girls when they come home. I need to somehow to tell Peter. God, he is going to hate me. I hate hurting people, but there is no other way around it. It's not going to work with him.

"Okay," I say as I look back into his eyes. He smiles, gets out of his chair, kneels down in front of me, grabs my hand, and lovingly asks me, "Amy, will you marry me again?" My eyes tear up with joy and compassion. The family that is sitting with us at our table is waiting for my answer. "We will start slow and I will think about it." I say. I want to say yes, but even now I feel a little caution is good. "I will go back to the Richardson name upon my divorce from Peter." "Fair enough" he says. "I love you so much Amy." The family sitting with us claps and raises their glasses to a toast. Nick and I raise our glasses too. "Cheers to you guys.

You make a beautiful couple." Nick and I look at each other and we both shed a couple tears of joy.

My conversation with the girls didn't go exactly the way that I wanted it to. They are not thrilled about this decision that I have made. I promise them that this time will not be like the others. They do accept it though. Jessica is so easy going that she doesn't really care. Julienne on the other hand not so much. I can't blame her. I do tell them that we will once again be doing a lot of fun things and that I would be able to stay home with them every day. I'm sick of cleaning houses.

It is now time for me to tell Peter. He sleeps late since he works nights. He finally gets up to make his coffee. I walk into the kitchen slowly. I stand in front of him and just look at him. "What's up, you are acting strange. Why are you staring at me like that?" He asks. My stomach is turning. This is so much harder than I thought it would be. I can't get the words to come out. I'm frozen. "What?!" he asks again. "We need to talk." I say. "Not in front of the kids. Let's go into the garage." I say firmly. "What is going on Amy?" I know he senses something is really off and not in a good way. "Fine let's go. I have a really bad feeling by the way that you are acting."

He follows me into the garage. I feel like I am going to vomit. I look at him while I fidget back and forth. "I can't do this." I timidly say. "Do what? Come on Amy quit beating around the bush and spit it out!" "This is not going to work between us. I made a mistake. I was not ready to get married again. And, the bottom line, I am not over Nick." He now looks like he is ready to explode. "You have been talking to him, haven't you? Did you sleep with? What the fuck Amy! You are one very messed up individual. You put the pressure

on me to marry you. I have not felt right about it since the day we married. I am not in love with you. I love and care about you, but I am not in love with you. I am so sorry. ""
Ha, you have some way of showing it. You are so fucked up in the head. I can't believe that you are still in love with that asshole after everything he has done to you and your children. He beat the shit out of you. Do you really think he has changed? Fuck this. I'm out of here. You can figure out how to pay the rent and the rest of the bills. I'm sure Nick will be more than happy to help you out." He stares at me with hatred in his eyes. "I don't need this bullshit. My friends tried to warn me. I should have listened. After everything that I have done for you and your kids? Seriously! I'm sorry that I don't have the money to wine and dine you all of the time like Nick, but I have loved you through all of this and gave you everything that I could. You are so selfish and such a bitch. He can have you! I'll be at my mom's until the weekend. Boy this is going to be humiliating telling her too. I am such a schmuck. I want you and the kids to be gone then so that I can move my stuff out of here. He walks down the stairs and slams the door behind him. He leaves for work.

I feel terrible, but I am somewhat relieved. I don't have to hide this anymore. I'm glad that I got it out. I'm glad that he will be staying at his mom's too. I will have to give Tyler to Nick right now so that I can still work while the kids are in school. I'm sure that he will give me some money to get by and so I will be able to figure the logistics out. I know that we will be moving back to Rochelle in the near future, but I have to do this the right way. I have to make sure the girls are going to be able to handle the move. Once again, I will have to reroute them to a new school.

WE MOVE AGAIN

ick and I are having dinner with all of the kids at Chucky Cheese. They all are having a great time. Marley is here with us. I have missed her. My three girls are together once again. You can see how happy they are. "Dad, can we have some money now for our tokens?" Marley asks him. He gives them each $10.00 and asks them to look over their little brother. "I need to talk to mom about something." He says. I notice that he says "Mom" and not "your mom." It's just like the old days.

"It's time to help you move honey. I found us a cute house to rent for a while in Rockford. I already paid six months on the lease. This will give us time to look for a new permanent house together. We will be making new beginnings and new memories. The old house is up for sale." He shows me pictures. It's a cute white cape cod style house in a cozy little subdivision. "I like it. It's cute." I say. "I have the keys and I want to take you and the kids over there tonight to check it out." Really?" I ask with some excitement. "This is all very exciting." We hug each other and start looking for the kids. "There they are." I say pointing to the skee ball area. "Hey kids! You about ready to cash in your tickets. It's time to go. I have a big surprise for you." Nick says to them.

The house is adorable. There are hardwood floors throughout the house. The upstairs bedrooms have cubby areas under the windows that meet each other as part of storage and closet space. I don't for see it being used for storage, but rather a club house for the girls to play in. I know that I would want to do that if I was still a child. "Which room do you guys want?" Julienne asks Marley and Jessica. The rooms are both the same. It's just a matter of which side of the house they want to be on. Jessica and Marley pick the left room beside the drive way. They are dancing around with excitement and talking about where all of their things are going to go. They love it. I do not see any stress here. Tyler will get the front little room downstairs that would normally be a dining room. Nick and I will take the back family room for our bedroom. It's not a big house like we have been used to, but it's very cozy and adorable. It has great decorating potential. There is a basement that Nick brings us down to look at. Half of it is finished. It's a great place for the kids to hang out, watch television, and play video games with their friends. The other side of the basement gives you an idea of how old the house is. It's actually pretty spooky. There is a large old boiler that has these scary trap doors. I feel like we are in a dungeon. It has an old creepy closet for storage. This is also where the washer and dryer are kept. I think that I will stick to the day time to do laundry. We have a small fenced in back yard and a one car garage which is where I'm sure that Nick will store extra water treatment equipment. "I really like it. It's perfect." I say with a smile. "The girls seem to love it too." "I knew you would like it. It's small, but it's temporary. It's a fresh start."

We are moved in. Everyone is happy. The girls are doing okay in their new schools. They have already made some new friends. The girls have seemed to adjust quite quickly and well. Nick has been great. He has been very loving toward all of us. We spend a lot of time together as a family now. I am back at home running the household, being a mom, and feel some sense of pride once again. Life is good and I just wish that my parents could be happy for us too. They can't believe that I am back with Nick and will not have anything to do with us. It's a shame because they are not spending any time with their grandchildren. I will just have to give it time so that I can prove that everything is going to be okay this time.

It's a Saturday morning. Nick decides he is going to make us a big breakfast. He makes eggs, bacon, sausage, and toast. I walk into the kitchen to see what he is making. "Honey you know that the girl's don't like eggs." I say. "Ya, well they are scrambled. They can eat them just fine." My gut instantly sinks. All I can think is oh no. Please don't force the girls to eat eggs again. Why would he make them this for breakfast? What is wrong with pancakes? He brings in the food for all of us into the other room. He sets everyone's plate down in front of each of us. Julienne immediately, "Nick you know that I don't like eggs." Jessica then makes her comment that she doesn't like them either. "Can we have something else?" Jessica asks very kindly. Marley has no problem nor does Tyler. They start eating right away. I can see the look on Nick's face. He is angry. I'm not feeling very good about this. Please don't lose it Nick. "These are not wet and yokey. Don't waste food. Eat your breakfast with some respect." He says in a stern tone. I can see Julienne's defiance begin in her mind from her body language and the expression. Nick looks right back at her and says, "Fine Julienne, you will be sitting at this table until you eat your food. This could be a very long day for you." "NO!" She yells back firmly. Nick now grabs her by the arm and pulls her out of her chair. "Julienne, I am not going to put up with this attitude of yours. Let's go!"" Nick, please stop, it's only eggs." I say. At this point there was no stopping him. Once he is in this mood caution must be made on how to talk to him. He is pulling her to the doorway of the basement and she is fighting the tears, but not doing a very good job of it. This is what Nick wants. He wants to make her cry and make a point to all of us. "Nick come on. Please stop this. Let her go hungry until dinner or something."" Amy, stay out of this. She needs to learn a lesson. I will not put up with this attitude of hers. She is not in control of this house. She needs to do as she is told. It is time for her to learn some manners once and for all." I feel helpless. I'm afraid to say or do anything in fear of making the situation worse. He throws Julienne over his shoulder and carries her down the basement stairs. I hear the downstairs door slam. Nick returns upstairs and says, "Now we can all eat." Jessica is all out bawling. She can't control the tears. She can't eat because she is too upset. "Jessica is this a problem with you too?" He yells at her. Nick does the same with her. Now they are both downstairs locked in the basement. I try to get up to run down to them. "Amy, don't even think about it. Stay here. They need to learn." "You would never do this to Marley or Tyler." I say. "Why are you doing this to my girls?" I am crying now as well. What is happening right now? Things have been going so well. "Marley and Tyler are eating their food. There is no reason to punish them." "Ya well they like eggs and they are your flesh and blood." I snap back. He then pulls me hard by my arm and lifts me off of my chair. He is dragging me into the kitchen. He pushes me into the wall, holds me there, and yells at me. "Amy don't you ever under mind me like that again. Your kids need to be taught a lesson period. Get that?" I'm afraid to say anything else and just nod my head in agreement.

It's been an hour and the girls are still locked up downstairs. I want to run down to them. What will he do to me? Marley is quiet and just watches television while Tyler is playing in his room with his lego set. I can't take this anymore. Nick suddenly says that he has to run to the office for a while. Thank God I think to myself. Get the fuck out of here please. As soon as his van is headed down the street I run downstairs. Marley follows me down. Nick locked them in the spooky side of the basement. The door is locked. I unlock it, open the door, and see Jessica is sitting on the washing machine crying. "Where is your sister?" Jessica points to the closed closet door. What the fuck? He locked Julienne into that pitch black closet. I yank open the closet door to see Julienne sitting on the floor crying. "Oh my God. I am so sorry honey." How could I let him do this? "We don't like eggs mommy." Jessica is crying to me. I hold her tight in my arms. "I know sweetie. You didn't do anything wrong. I am going to make you guys something else to eat. Better yet, let's go to McDonalds for some pancakes. You guys can all play for a while. We could all use some time out of here" Julienne looks at me and wipes her tears and says, "Okay." Marley asks me, "Do you think that my dad will be mad if we go?" "Honey I do not care at this point. He had no right to do this. I will speak with your dad later."

I watch the kids play in the tunnels. I keep replaying what had just happened in my mind. At least the girls seem to be having fun now like nothing ever happened which is calming me. I can't believe he went off like this. What have I done? He can't stand it when Julienne stands up to him. It hurts his ego. I know it. He is going to get a mouthful from me tonight. I will not stand for this.

We make it back home. Tyler goes back to his room to play with his Legos and cars. The girls get themselves engrossed in a Disney movie. I start prepping tonight's dinner. Nick walks in the back door happy like nothing never happened here. "Sold another deal honey." He comes up to me and grabs my ass. "How about a quickie to celebrate?" I push his hands off of me and turn to look him in the eyes. "I don't think so." I say sternly. "What's wrong?" He asks. "How can you even ask me that question right now?" I snap back. "What, because I gave the girls a time out? Julienne especially needs to learn to adjust her attitude." "Nick! A time out is (go up to your room), not locking small children in a dark cold basement. And shit especially locking a child in a dark scary closet! You terrified them for God's sake! What is wrong with you? Don't you ever do that again!"

His anger is building. I can see it in his eyes and posture. He starts his little agitated dance back and forth trying to control himself. He fidgets and now puts his hands on his hips. He actually holds himself back and keeps his mouth shut. I am expecting an apology at this point. His ego won't allow him to do so. His phone rings. Wow saved by the bell. He is talking to one of his employees about an installation going wrong. "I'll be there in thirty minutes." He says to one of his guys and then hangs up. He quickly walks into the living room and apologizes to both of the girls. Jessica nods that it's okay. Julienne folds her arms and looked away. Nick then turns and walks out the door without saying goodbye.

Wow, I actually stood up to him and he controlled himself. The damage is still done. I'm very worried about Julienne and him ever getting along. This will cause a lot of tension in the home. How can I blame her for how she feels? Once again her mother has failed her. I try to comfort the kids with a nice dinner. Nick is not here and it's just us. I'm glad that he is not here right now. This gives everyone some time to relax before bed. When Nick gets like this, which I never thought that it would happen again, I just want him to stay away from us.

The kids went to bed about an hour ago. Everyone is asleep, but me of course. Nick finally walks in the back door at eleven o'clock. I'm watching a Life Time movie on the couch. He walks into the living room and says, "Hi Amy." with a very cold tone. He looks at me for a moment and then just turns away. I hear him in the kitchen making a rum and coke while he talks to himself. I'm not sure what he is saying and honestly I don't want to know. He does talk to himself a lot. He will have full length conversations. I turn off the television and head into the bedroom. I'm mentally drained from this horrible day. I need to be up early tomorrow to take Julienne to the orthodontist. She is in her first round of treatment to expand the roof of her mouth. I have to crank this little key inside of her mouth every week so it will gradually widen itself. She has an actual piece inside of her mouth that is called an expander. She will have to have a bone grafting surgery from her hip and put into the roof of her mouth next year. She has little bone mass where her cleft palate was. More bone mass has to be created to allow any oral reconstruction.

The next morning, we are all up early. Julienne has a mouth expander support piece that she is supposed to wear as often as possible. This speeds up the process to get her mouth to expand. When she is at home or asleep she needs to wear it. This morning in particular she refuses to wear it. She is getting red sore marks on her face from wearing it. It is uncomfortable and she wants to get a break from wearing it. Nick sees that she is not wearing it and immediately starts to yell at her to put it back on. "It's hurting my face." She says. "It won't work unless you keep it on and it's costing us a lot of money that I don't want to see run down the drain." He replies. "Nick please, she is going to the orthodontist today. Let her take a break from it. Her face has sores on it and it's painful." I intervene. "No, we are paying a lot of money for this. She needs to wear it now!" he yells. Julienne breaks into tears and puts it back on. "Jesus Nick. You are being mean and unreasonable. "He snaps at me. "Oh, really? Maybe when her lowlife father steps in to pay for it I won't be so mean." Julienne runs upstairs to her room. "You do not need to say things like that in front of her. None of this is her fault. I'm sorry that Scott does not help out. I have done all that I can to get him to pay legally. I remember a time when you wouldn't give me child support for Tyler and you actually had the money to do so." Oh God what did I just do? I really pissed him off by saying that. Nick gets in my face and starts poking hard into my chest with his finger and says, "You would never make it without me. You should be grateful and so should she. I work my ass off and get no respect!" With each poke of his finger my eyes blink in fear. "Please stop it. You are scaring me. That hurts." I cry out to him. He turns around and heads over to the coffee pot. While he is talking to himself he grabs the wet coffee grounds out of the coffee maker and throws them all over the kitchen floor. He then grabs the empty coffee pot and throws it at the wall. Glass is shattering everywhere. All of the kids come running into the kitchen with terrified looks on their faces. I immediately walk them out of the kitchen. I tell the girls that I am okay and to just get ready for school. I want to get them out the door as soon as possible. I am not sure where this is going, but I am not feeling very good about it. I can't trust him when he is like this. "I need to get the girls off to school." I say to him quietly. I don't want to agitate him anymore than he already is. I need to let him calm down. I'm scared and I am starting to cry, but I turn and walk away to help get the kids ready. Nick comes after me and grabs me by my hair. "You leave the room when I say you can leave the room." He says to me. "Nick please stop. You are hurting me and you are scaring the kids." "Good, you all need to learn a lesson. I am in charge of this house. Clean up this mess now." I am too terrified to not do as he says. I stoop down to start picking up the large pieces of glass and throw them in the garbage.

The girls come down to say they are ready for school. They see the distress that I am in. I know that they are scared. "You two get going. I am okay. Don't worry. I want you to have a nice day at school. Julienne don't forget that I will be picking you up from school at 11:00 for your appointment. They both just stand there frozen in fear. I get up and walk them to the front door. "Julienne once you are down the street a bit, go ahead and take this thing off of your face and put it in your backpack. I know it's hurting you honey. It's okay to take it off." I say very quietly so Nick does not hear me say this. I send them on their way. They are both crying and they keep turning around to look back at me. I'm really worried about the school questioning them. I don't want to lose my girls again.

Oh crap. Tyler is running around in bare feet. I can't let him go into the kitchen. Where is he? Oh thank God, he is playing with his toys on our bed. My adrenaline is kicking into full force. I'm shaking and scared, but I go back into the kitchen and see Nick standing over the sink talking to himself. He is justifying what he just did. I want to hit him. I want to scream at him. But, I don't in fear of what he may do. I know what could happen if I do. I just stare at him instead and wait.

"I'm sorry Amy. I lost it." Now he starts to cry. I know that things are still financially hard while he is getting his business going again. I try to rationalize his behavior in my head. I'm not really sure what to say or do. "I understand. I know that you are under a lot of pressure and didn't mean it." I say in return. The truth is that I don't really understand, but it's what he wants to hear right now and it will help him to calm down. I carefully start once again to pick up the pieces of glass while my mind just races. I need to just stay calm. I hated sending the girls to school like that. He promised me that he was better now. I am questioning if he has relapsed on the drugs. Right now I just want him to get out of here and go to work. He looks at me and says, "I am going to work. I want to make this up to you. How about we take the kids to a movie tonight? I will sit down and talk to them later and tell them how sorry that I am and that I would never hurt their mother. I will make this right, I promise." Before he walks out the door he kneels down and gently cradles my face. "Amy I love you very much. Do you still love me?" "Yes Nick, I still love you. Let's start over with no more tantrums. We need to talk about our feelings before it gets to this point. You scare the kids and I when you are like this. I just got my daughters back. I do not want to lose them again. "I know, I am so sorry. This is unforgivable. I am trying so hard to control myself. I don't know what gets into me sometimes." He says as more tears are running down his face. "I have to make this right and I will. I promise." "Let's get ourselves back to church like you promised." I say. "Okay." He agrees and heads out the door to work.

The glass is now picked up. I stare out the kitchen window in a daze. I feel exhausted. I'm lost, nervous, and scared. My thoughts are all over the place. My stomach is turning. I want to vomit. I decide to get dressed and make myself presentable. My eyes are swollen and red. The makeup isn't helping at all. I'm so worried about my girls right now. I promised them this would never happen again. I failed them. Lord please help me. I have to stay strong for me my children.

HONEYMOON PHASE
ONCE AGAIN OR
SO I THOUGHT

ick has really been putting in the effort to change his ways. He is being the man that he should be for his family. Everyone has relaxed and gotten back to normal. Marley comes running down the stairs and asks me, "When do we get to start making the pizzas?" "We are waiting for your dad to get home. We are supposed to do this as a family." It's now seven o'clock. I'm sure the kids are getting hungry, "Is he on his way? We are getting really hungry." She says. "How about I cut up some fruit with some dip to hold you guys over?" She rolls her eyes and says, "Okay" in frustration. Nick did say that he'd be home by six tonight. He's late and he has not called. He knows that we are all waiting on him. Now I'm getting aggravated. I call his cell phone. After several rings I get his voicemail. I decide to leave him a message. "Ya, hon you are late and we have not heard from you. The kids are patiently waiting for you to get home so we can make pizzas. Can you please call me back so I know what is going on?" I hang up. I feel like something is not right here. In the past if he did not answer he was out using. He normally is so good about being in touch. I want to be wrong. I really hope that history is not repeating itself. It's going to take me a long time to let go and trust that there will be no relapse.

It's now eight 'clock. I try to call him again. He does not answer so I leave another message. "Nick seriously, what is going on? A phone call would be appreciated. I guess the kids and I are making pizzas without you." I call the kids down. "Where's my dad?" Marley asks. "I have no idea. I don't know about you guys, but I'm starving. Let's get started on these pizzas." We have our little pizza party and some ice cream for dessert. We watch Sponge Bob episodes together until we all could no longer hold our eyes open. It's midnight. There has still been no word from Nick. I'm very angry now. This is not a good sign at all. When he avoids me it has always been because of using cocaine. Fuck it. I'm tired and I'm going to bed. I'm drifting off to sleep and the phone awakens me. Oh God, something has happened I think to myself. I answer and it's Jennifer on the other line. "Amy I am sorry to wake you, but you need to know that Nick was just here beating on my door. I did not answer because I know he is out of his mind on coke. You need to be prepared. I'm worried because Marley is with you." "Well

I must say that I am not surprised. I knew something was up when he blew us off tonight and was not answering my calls. I am dreading when he comes home. I hope he stays away tonight. All of the kids are asleep otherwise I would bring Marley home." "I'm having problems with my car right now." She tells me. "Please call me when you get up in the morning or if anything happens before then. If he doesn't cause you any problems can you bring Marley home then? I don't want her there when he is like this. Damn him! I was going to ask him for some help financially to get my car fixed too." "I will do my best to get her home as soon as possible. If things get bad around here I will call the police. I am so pissed at him myself. Has he tried to come on to you lately? Just tell me the truth." "Yes he has. He stopped here last week when Marley was at school. He had me against the hallway door with his fingers up inside me. I'm sorry. I told him to stop, but he wouldn't. He threatened me to keep my mouth shut or he would cut me off. He leaves money on my kitchen table if I keep quiet." "Jesus, how many times?" "Too many to count. I am so sorry Amy. He is sick. I hate the fact that I need his help to make it. I have been put on a lot of medication for depression because of him." I am wide awake now. I am heartbroken. I just ruined my life for him and now I am stuck. I have nowhere to go. Everyone I love has walked out of my life because I went back to him. I have no idea what to do at this point. We hang up and just sit there on my bed. I cry until I can no longer shed any more tears. I am so stupid. I punch the pillows and then throw them across the room. One of them hit one of our photos and broke the glass into fine pieces.

It's one thirty in the morning now and I'm still awake. I

go sit on the couch in the dark and stare into the blackness of the room. The back door opens. I hear Nick shuffling around in the kitchen. I hear him making himself a cocktail. How should I handle this? I stay sitting on the couch. He walks into the room and turns on the light to see me sitting there staring ahead. "Hi honey." He says. I look up at him with hate in my eyes. "Where have you been? I was trying to reach you all night. Are you using again?" "I had to work late. Sorry I was busy." So busy that you could not let me know what was going on while I sit here in wonder and worry? How would you like it if I did that to you? Did you go to Jennifer's tonight?" "No, why would I go there?" "She called me tonight. Do you still want to lie to me? Oh and wait this was not the first time? Was she a good fuck? I hate you so much right now." "Okay I have been over there. I have been trying to help her. She came on to me." "I don't care who did what first at this point. The point is you have been lying to me and fucking her." It's that instant he loses it. He slaps me so hard that I fall to the ground. "Don't you ever speak to me that way again. You need me. You are stuck with me now. I can do whatever I want on my free time. "He walks away to go upstairs. He wakes Marley and carries her down the stairs. He then grabs Tyler out of his bed and wraps a blanket around him. He takes them out to the car, gets them strapped in and then comes back in. He walks into the bedroom. I am still on the floor holding my face. He lifts me up with both of his arms and throws me against the wall. He has a choke hold on me. I can't breathe. He stares me in the eyes and chokes me harder. I can't speak. I can't do anything. Am I going to die right here and now? My daughters are upstairs and they are going to come down to a dead mom. I lift my knee and slam it into his balls as hard as I can. He lets me go. I'm gasping for air. "I'm taking my kids out of here." He says. "Let's see how you like that. This will teach you a lesson." He turns his back and starts to walk away. I scream at him. "You mother fucker!" I grab the vase that is sitting next to me on our dresser. Without even thinking I slam the vase on his head. He falls to the floor. I kick him over and over again. I kick him in the legs, arms, and his head. This force has come over me. My adrenaline is flowing through my veins. He is not moving. The girls come running down the stairs. "Mom! What is happening?" They turn the corner to see Nick lying on the floor. They stare in disbelief. They are frozen. I look at them as if to say I'm sorry. I lost control. "Your brother and sister are in the car outside. Please bring them back in and go upstairs. I need to call the police. I have no feeling inside. I am numb beyond words. Maybe he is dead. I don't give a shit. This was the last time he was going to do this to me.

The police arrive and Nick is still not moving. I open the front door in a daze. I point to the kitchen without even saying a word. I'm in shock. Nick is pronounced dead on the scene. One of the officers goes upstairs to check on my children and to talk to them. Blood is running down my face. I didn't even realize that he cracked my skull after he slapped me so hard and banged my head against the wall in the choke hold. I have black and blue strangle marks on my neck. I can't speak. The officers are trying to get my statement, but I can't get the words out. They can see that I fought for my life. I am not being arrested. I am taken on a gurney and put into the ambulance. I can hear my girls crying. "Mommy!" I turn towards their voices. "Mam, don't worry. We are going to take care of the children and make sure they are safe. We need to get you to the hospital.

I wake up in the hospital. My head hurts so bad. I have a bandage wrapped around it. My right arm is in a cast. I feel sedated. "Hi sweetie." It's my mother's voice. I look over at her. She looks exhausted. She has been crying. I realize where I am at and why. "I'm so sorry mom." I say to her while my eyes are welling up with tears. "I should have listened to you." "Don't worry honey. You don't have to say another word. We love you and everything is going to be okay. He will never hurt you again. You are a fighter." "The kids. Where are the kids? Are they okay?" "Arthur, you can bring them in now." She says with a smile. My dad walks in with Tyler, Julienne, and Jessica safe and sound. They all give me hugs. "We are taking care of them. You just get yourself better. You have a pretty bad head injury so you have to camp out here for a while." "I killed him mom." I am crying so hard now. "Am I going to jail?" "No honey. This was obviously self- defense. You are lucky to be alive. There are no charges against you. You are safe. He can't hurt you anymore."

t is so hard for those on the outside to understand what an abused woman goes through. It's a painful roller coaster of love and hate. An abuser knows what to say and do at the right time to keep you. You forgive over and over again believing that this time will be different. You love them and want to believe they are still a good person. You find reasons or excuses for their behavior. You believe that you can fix them. You are dependent on them for financial resource. To all of you women out there who have been abused, I hope my story helps you. You are not alone. You are stronger than you think you are. Get the help that you need to stay strong. You don't need to stay in the relationship. They will not change. It's who they are. Abuse is not okay. There is help out there. Reach out to a therapy group. There are resources to help you get on your feet. Your life and your children's lives are worth it. You deserve better. I love you all.

Printed in the United States
by Baker & Taylor Publisher Services